A Life Lived Outdoors

Reflections of a Maine Sportsman

We love the outdoors! More great titles from Islandport Press.

Backtrack
By V. Paul Reynolds

This Cider Still Tastes Funny! and *Suddenly, the Cider Didn't Taste So Good!*
By John Ford Sr.

Birds of a Feather and *Tales from Misery Ridge*
By Paul Fournier

Where Cool Waters Flow
By Randy Spencer

My Life in the Maine Woods
By Annette Jackson

Nine Mile Bridge
By Helen Hamlin

These and other books are available at:
www.islandportpress.com.

Islandport Press is a dynamic, award-winning publisher
dedicated to stories rooted in the essence and sensibilities of
New England. We strive to capture and explore the grit, beauty,
and infectious spirit of the region by telling tales, real and
imagined, that can be appreciated in many forms by readers,
dreamers, and adventurers everywhere.

A Life Lived Outdoors

Reflections of a Maine Sportsman

By George Smith

ISLANDPORT PRESS

Islandport Press
P.O. Box 10
247 Portland Street
Yarmouth, Maine 04096
www.islandportpress.com
books@islandportpress.com

ISBN: 978-1-934031-59-9
Library of Congress Card Number: 2013922642

Dean L. Lunt, publisher
Book jacket design, Karen F. Hoots, Hoots Design
Book design, Michelle A. Lunt
Cover photograph, Hilary Smith
Back cover photograph courtesy of George Smith

To Linda Hillier Smith

While she doesn't usually like me to write about her,
she is right there, often beside me, more often leading the way.
Even when she walks behind me, she's in front of me,
in my head and my heart.

What's in this book?

After writing more than 850,000 words for his newspaper editorial column, over a twenty-two-year period, George Smith had plenty to offer for this edition, a collection of his favorite columns. He set aside the political columns (not the favorites of his readers, he says) for those about home and camp, family and friends, life in rural Maine, and hunting, fishing, and other outdoor fun. You will also find a few columns that appeared in *Down East* magazine, and some that George wrote especially for this book.

Contents

Foreword

This book is a long valentine to the hills, small towns, back roads, woods, ponds, and streams (especially the streams) of George Smith's native state. They conjure up images of a simpler time, when a boy would study the elusive mysteries of the trout or the habits of woodcock and grouse, and the nearest thing to a video game was *The Price is Right*. All of the essays involve people, often members of George's family, but the real protagonist is always Maine—and it's his passion for the place that drives each small story.

What struck me was the image implicit throughout the book of Maine as teacher—teacher of skills and useful knowledge, of character and patience, of life principles, but mostly, as teacher of values. Respect for others (even people who don't like hunting), a flinty integrity, simplicity, and above all, a profound sense of stewardship of the natural gifts Maine offers. Those of us lucky enough to live here often take this quality for granted, especially amid the clamor of everyday life. But George brings it to life—brings Maine to life—in a way that is direct, clear, often touching, and always true.

Napoleon once famously observed that war is history; Freud's counter was that anatomy is destiny. But this little book suggests a third formulation: that geography is character. Maine is a tough place and always has been; even in the twenty-first century, we have to keep a weather eye cocked lest high water, a nor'easter, or whiteout on the turnpike catch us unawares. There's a sense of the place that it doesn't give much willingly, that its benefits have to be earned, and thus earned, are all the more valuable.

In the end, what the book made me realize is how much Maine has worked its way into each of us, defining who we are, how we see the world, and, most importantly, what we value.

My only complaint is that George didn't tell us where those brookies are.

—US Senator Angus King
September 2013

Introduction

My first review for this collection was a pisser. Literally. The cat peed on and tore up my newspaper columns, spread around the floor during the review and selection process for this book, perhaps his commentary on the content. I hope you enjoy it more than he did.

When Doug Rooks, the first of my dozen editors, hired me twenty-two years ago to write a weekly column for the *Kennebec Journal*, he said he didn't care what I wrote about, as long as I stirred people up. Turns out I've got a natural talent for that.

While many of the issues are perennial, the technology of writing this column has changed dramatically. At the start, I wrote the column on a yellow legal pad, typed it on an electric typewriter, then drove to Augusta to deliver it to the paper, where someone else retyped it.

These days I bang it out on my laptop and whip it to the paper via e-mail. I don't really understand how that works, but it sure makes writing a whole lot easier and more enjoyable.

After an estimated 850,000 words, it was surprisingly easy to pick my favorites. Even though the column appears on the editorial page, and I did pontificate about politics and weighty issues on a regular basis, it's the columns about the outdoors, family, camp, hunting, fishing, and other outdoor activities and issues that seemed to resonate most with readers. You get plenty of those here.

You will also notice that most columns focus on one thing: me. Linda presented me with a T-shirt last Christmas that lists my website, www.georgesmithmaine.com, on the front, and says on the back: IT'S ALL ABOUT ME. And it is. Maine, that is—and me, too.

I write in the first person, using far more "I"s than my writing professors at the University of Maine would ever have allowed. Well, I've used it eight times so far just in this introduction!

Doug Rooks and I came up with the title for my column, "The Native Conservative," but I've never liked it. Yes, I'm a native Mainer, and suppose that gives me a certain perspective. And yes, I'm conservative, but not in the ferocious, doctrinaire way that some choose to display their thoughts.

While I've read that most people grow more conservative as they age (and accumulate things), I've grown more liberal—or at least more tolerant. I used to hate change; now I am amused by it, even as I continue to resist. So last October, we changed the name of my column to "Maine Stream." That's where I reside today.

If you are holding this book in your hand, you may be like me. No computer tablets for us! And I thank you for that. And if you are reading this on a tablet, well, I have to thank you too.

Please know that I enjoy hearing from readers, even if I wrote something you disagree with, and can be reached at georgesmithmaine.com, or the old-fashioned way, at 34 Blake Hill Road, Mount Vernon, Maine 04352.

Part I:
Home, Camp, and Maine Life

Camp Is a Maine Tradition

Every Mainer has a camp. It may be a place we own. It may be a place our friends own. It may be a place we rent every summer. It may even be a campground and simple tent. But it's ours, even if only for a week or two each year.

Camp is a Maine tradition—anchored in our imaginations of the North Woods, yet often nearby on a lake or pond, the better to access it on hot summer days. I know one couple whose camp is a hundred yards behind their house on a man-made pond.

Camp may be rustic with a two-holer. It may have plumbing and hot showers. It may have a kitchen or just a Coleman stove on the picnic table. It may be on the water or deep in the woods. But it is always the most comfortable place on Earth.

Our camp is tucked just outside the northwest corner of Baxter Park on Nesowadnehunk Lake. It was once part of a well-known sporting camp. It is a place of wild critters, eager trout, and many mountains—quiet, peaceful, relaxing, restorative. And yes, of running water and hot showers. Camp is a key component of our quality of life and mental health.

Camp is lying in bed at night and listening to the haunting cry of a loon. It's looking out the window as you enjoy a steaming cup of coffee in the morning and seeing a moose amble on by.

Camp is an Adirondack chair, knotty pine walls, old furniture, and sitting up late playing cards or going to bed early, as soon as the sun sets.

At our camp, we've barbecued outside while watching a brood of young rabbits race each other 'round and 'round our picnic table; picked wild berries, keeping a close eye out for bears; and paddled a fast stream in our kayaks, getting knocked completely out of our craft by a "widow-maker."

Camp is a wild brook trout caught on a fly or a smallmouth bass on a spinning lure; a hike up a mountain or a stroll along the beach; a gorgeous magnolia warbler in your binoculars or a big black bear coming toward you in the road.

Camp is for kids—of all ages—dangling worms at the end of a hook with a grandchild, hoping for a white perch; splashing in the water on hot summer days; playing lawn games; and, of course, cooking s'mores over an open fire. Chocolate never tasted so good.

Camp is bean-hole beans, pancakes, eggs and bacon. For some, it's venison from last fall's deer. Camp may be the place you go every year to hunt deer or upland birds, or to fish.

For me, camp is the sun rising over Strickland Mountain, which lurks over the left shoulder of our camp, enjoyed in solitude from the boat as I whip a dry fly toward feeding trout; it's a hot cup of the darkest coffee, grounds scouring the bottom of my cup, as soon as I get in from fishing; and it's blueberry pancakes with real maple syrup from our Mount Vernon neighbors, followed by a bowl of strawberries picked the day before along the trail behind camp.

Camp for my family is two does galloping all over the front lawn in the spring, kicking up their hooves after a long, confining winter; a cow moose escorting her calf past our camp toward the shore for a drink; a black duck with six ducklings hovering in the lee of our boat in the lagoon; a merganser

swimming past the beach with a dozen little 'gansers following, all in a row. It's also the heartache of seeing her each week
with fewer chicks, until she is left with a single one that she
guards with a desperate ferocity.

To get to camp you may drive, boat, bicycle, or walk. But
once you are there, you stay close to home. You revel in the
fact that "there is nothing to do."

I just love it when friends ask, "What on earth do you do up
there?"

You can't imagine. You must experience it to understand.

Camp is the family gathering for a traditional week every
summer at the lake, or just the two of you, tucked far away
from civilization. Or maybe even just you, enjoying a time of
quiet reflection with no distractions.

Camp is the place we read that stack of books we've been
saving.

Camp is no cell phone, computer, or television; often, it's
no electricity.

Well, perhaps you'll have electricity and all of these gadgets
(and more) at camp with you, but you can't hear the cry of the
loon if the TV set is blaring; you can't read a great mystery
while you are texting; and you can't get away from the office if
you carry it with you to camp.

Maine's camps and campgrounds are the cure for all that ails
you. Take the cure this year.

— My Maine column, *Down East* magazine (2011)

Nature at Peace

Woodchucks are one of the few wild critters Linda allows me to shoot in the yard. Anything that gets into her garden is fair game. This season, I shot two fat chucks, but a smaller one eluded me. Our cats would chase it around but never catch it.

Then our neighbor Dona came through. One week when we were at camp, she captured the woodchuck in a live trap and, kind soul that she is, transported it far away where it could live in the forest without annoying any home gardener—at least, that was the theory.

We'd had two blissful weeks of harvesting Lin's prolific garden without competition, when one day, I heard a knock on the door and opened it to find our young neighbor, Justin Brickett, and his beagle.

Always polite, Justin said, "Mr. Smith, I just saw a bald eagle flying up the road with a woodchuck. The woodchuck was heavy, and the eagle dropped it in the bushes just past your lawn."

Great. Now we've got eagles delivering woodchucks to us. Of course, the woodchuck did have a bad day, and it might not have survived the ordeal, but Justin and I couldn't find it in the bushes.

Whenever I encounter the "eat or be eaten" situation that exists in the wilds of Maine, I am reminded of conversations with Buzz Caverly, who often described Baxter Park as "nature at peace."

Nature is rarely at peace. It's a killing field out there.

Daughter Rebekah was at our camp on the edge of Baxter Park a few weeks ago when she heard screeching one night. Outside, she saw a huge great horned owl killing a rabbit on the lawn in front of camp. The owl flew up into a nearby tree and waited patiently for Becky to go back inside so he could enjoy his meal.

The next week, Linda and I found a baby bunny living in the woodpile beside our camp's fire pit on the front lawn. The bunny would come out during the day and lay in the grass next to the woodpile. Lin laid out a scrumptious meal for the bunny one day, but he chose to ignore it. He appeared to be healthy.

The morning we were to leave for home, Lin looked out the camp's front window and saw a large coyote sniffing around the woodpile, hoping for a breakfast bunny. We chased the coyote away, although he took his time and kept looking back wistfully in the direction of the woodpile. No doubt he was back soon after we left. That bunny didn't have a chance. We never saw it again.

We accept this, in the wilds. It's only when the wild critters invade what we consider our space that we really take notice.

Representative Mike Shaw, a Democrat from Standish, told me last spring that a weasel had gotten into his henhouse and killed forty-five chicks in one night, hauling them under the floor. The tiny weasel is a killing machine.

One Thanksgiving morning during a blizzard, we looked out the front kitchen window of our Mount Vernon home just in time to see a sharp-shinned hawk knock a blue jay off the feeder and to the ground. The hawk pecked away rapidly at the jay, blue feathers flying in all directions.

Lin couldn't watch. I, of course, was fascinated. Those blue feathers, flying up and into the cascading white snow, were kind of beautiful.

Over the years I have witnessed astonishing carnage in the fields and forests of Maine and beyond. One day while golfing in Florida, I saw a largemouth bass come right out of the water to snare a small bird.

For years, I hated snapping turtles after seeing one take a baby duck off the surface of the pond behind our house. Sportsmen hate coyotes that haul down deer and start cruelly chewing on them while they're still alive.

But I've often enjoyed watching foxes "mousing" in the fields. They stalk quietly along in the tall grass, then jump high and pounce on the unsuspecting mouse. Of course, while I enjoy the spectacle, it's not so good for the mouse.

In Labrador, we fished with imitations of mice and voles, skittering them across the surface of the river until huge brook trout grabbed them. The trout up there eat a lot of voles that fall into the river.

A few years ago a woman in the Millinocket area captured on video a bear grabbing and lugging off a moose calf. All she could do was scream, "It's killing the baby! It's killing the baby!"

Ah, yes, but that's nature at peace.

—Central Maine Newspapers (2008)

Making Do in Maine

We make do in Maine. For those who have no idea what this means, *do* is not a product that we make. *Make do* is what we do.

The term *make-do* is actually in the dictionary, defined as "makeshift," a hyphenated adjective. *Makeshift* is a noun or adjective meaning, "A crude and temporary expedient: substitute."

They got it wrong. There is nothing temporary about making do. And it's more than an adjective; it's a permanent way of life—at least in Maine.

This occurred to me last winter as I noticed the cold seeping through the hole in the thumb of my right-hand glove. These gloves were only a year old, so I've been making do with them. It was nearing the end of January, so it seemed wasteful to buy a new pair. I decided to make do until spring.

Actually, I have an idea for making do with my gloves even longer. That idea came to me one time while watching my nephew, Nate Damm, playing basketball with one white and one black sneaker. He was not making do; these were new sneakers. Apparently mismatched colors are trendy.

So why not mismatched gloves? I have a closet full of single mittens and gloves, the mates lost or worn out. I've started mixing and matching them, and can make do for years to come.

This works for socks, too. It's just amazing how many times two matched socks can go into the laundry basket and only one return to my bureau drawer. Now I am making do with mismatches.

9

Making do sometimes means aligning yourself with fate and taking whatever comes your way without complaint. I once backed out of the garage right into the side of a friend's automobile. This is not that unusual. Twice I've backed out of the garage right through the garage door. If God had wanted me to look back, He'd have put eyes in the back of my head.

In the case of my friend's car, my vehicle was unharmed, but her car sported a deep dent in the left rear fender. When I apologized and offered to pay for the repair, she said, "Oh, don't worry about it. We don't fix things like that." That's really making do, isn't it?

Daughter Hilary once hit a deer at the end of our road, leaving a long dent in the left front fender of her car. The fender was pushed back a bit so she couldn't open her driver's side door. I fixed that with a screwdriver, maneuvering the fender back into place. She made do with the dent.

My home office is a make-do kind of place. Pieces of the laminated side panels of my wooden desk are missing, and the front panels on the drawers are all loose, so that the things inside are constantly slipping through the cracks and falling out onto the floor.

I have four filing cabinets in three different colors, scavenged from who knows where. But they're all the same height, so we're making do. The radio on my desk once included a CD player, but that function no longer works. I can still get Maine Public Radio, so we're making do with it.

I was making do with a very old television in my office. None of the buttons on the TV worked, and the remote no longer could punch up any stations that required a zero, but otherwise—hey, it was good enough. Then Lin bought me a new office TV for Christmas, and now I'm getting all the channels. I've stored the old TV in the garage, if you want it.

Making do is really about sticking with the stuff that is good enough. It's frugality to the extreme. We don't throw much away, at least those of us with attics, garages, barns, or big yards. Someday that stuff will be useful, something we can make do with.

Of course, there are Mainers who don't make do. We bless them every time we go to the dump and cart home the "good-enough" stuff they discarded there.

You can tell the difference between the "making-do" Mainers and those that aren't, when each has a yard sale. There's nothing at all useful at the yard sale of a "making-do" Mainer.

Camp is where we really make do. A long crack in the middle pane of the window over our camp's kitchen sink is covered with duct tape. I broke the window ten years ago.

There's a lot we don't have at camp: no TV, no radio, no telephone (no cell-phone coverage), no closets, no electricity, no e-mail, no messages, no newspapers; no news at all.

We're making do.

— My Maine column, *Down East* magazine (2010)

Yard Sales—Triumph and Tragedy

A recent hilarious account of yard sales by J. P. Devine in this newspaper brought back a lot of memories—most of them bad. In 1998 my family hosted its first—and last—yard sale at our Mount Vernon home. Son Josh was sixteen and daughter Hilary thirteen at the time.

Our advertisement in the *Kennebec Journal* trumpeted 25 YEARS OF GREAT STUFF. But it was much more than that. An accumulation of items full of memories and personal history was offered up for sale.

It was a humbling experience. Josh predicted my old tape recorder wouldn't sell. Sure, it was in pieces. But that machine recorded, from the TV, Richard Nixon's 1964 acceptance speech at the Republican National Convention. With former president Eisenhower on his deathbed, that was Nixon's "Let's win this one for Ike" speech. And the tape went with the recorder. Alas, no takers.

Imagine standing behind a table with your worldly prizes spread out before you—things you had lovingly cherished and stored for many years, many offered at only a buck apiece—and having someone ask if you'd accept fifty cents.

Imbeciles! Okay, I didn't say that. But what was wrong with these people? Had they no sense of history?

I spread out six copies of Bill Cohen's first campaign brochure, used in his initial run for Congress in 1972. On page 5 was a photo of Bill and me on the steps of Bangor's City Hall. That was the campaign where I learned the political game as Bill's driver. At the end of the long, hot, and discouraging day,

I still had five of the six copies of that historic brochure left. I had given one away.

I gazed longingly at Hilary's table, where books and cute, cuddly stuffed animals were selling like hotcakes. Even her baked cookies were selling.

Josh's table was doing well with used sporting goods and games. And Linda seemed to have a lock on the market with her old stuff, from sneakers to cookware. She even offered each child a free book. Maybe I should have done something like that. No way. Not for nothing were they getting my good stuff.

I learned early in the day that I'm not very good at bargaining. After a couple of hours of very slow sales, I began to wonder what I was going to do with this yard full of stuff if it didn't sell. I cut prices quickly. Shortly after selling an outdoor set of table and four chairs for $25 and leaving it in the yard with a SOLD sign on it, someone came up and said, "You didn't sell that whole set for twenty-five dollars, did you? I'd have paid fifty."

That sure made me feel better.

It really was odd. Things I was sure would sell—the old church pew; an electric refrigerator in excellent shape; a good color television for $10; a huge L.L. Bean screen tent in good shape that originally sold for nearly $300, and was offered for only $125; top-of-the-line cross-country skis for just $35— garnered no interest.

Other things I considered junk were scarfed up: old records, computer equipment, boots; even our outdoor grill that I'd failed to clean after it was last used two years before.

Finally, about midday, I hit the jackpot. A lady from across town took an interest in our old wood-burning cookstove, the one I bought for $250 about ten years earlier, planning to use it in a camp someday. We already had one in our house.

When her husband returned later and agreed the stove was a beauty, I made the sale—for the same $250 I'd paid for it. Lin praised my excellent investment.

Apparently these sales go better in urban areas. Traffic was meager on our back road in Mount Vernon, although we had customers steadily throughout the day. Astonishingly, many cruised through the yard, eyeing hundreds of supremely valuable items offered at bargain prices, and walked away empty-handed. By the end of the day, I was begging people to take anything, for free.

Getting ready for this ordeal took a week of sweat in the hot attic, digging in the detritus of a lifetime. For every load of stuff that went into the sale, another load went to the dump. That's the only good thing about a yard sale, I guess; it does clean things out. Although I immediately began filling up that space with more memories.

I told Linda recently that it was time to have another yard sale. It's been fifteen years since the last one. You can guess what she said.

—Central Maine Newspapers (June 5, 2013)

Update: A few days after this was published, a guy from New Vineyard called to ask if I still had the L.L. Bean screen tent. I told him I did, and that he could have it for $75. He said he'd be over the next weekend to pick it up. I got it down from the attic and aired it out. When he didn't show up, I called him. He'd changed his mind.

History Slides By on Hopkins Stream

You stand on the side of Hopkins Stream beside the Blake Hill Road bridge, preparing to launch your canoe where Ron and Nancy LaRue generously provide public access to the stream. Admiring the LaRues' handsome brick house across the road, you don't know that those bricks were made just a few hundred yards away at the foot of Minnehonk Lake, behind my house. An old kiln and hundreds of discarded bricks litter the woods there.

Perhaps you gaze upstream, unaware of the box and board factory and the tannery that stood at each end of a dam there. The box factory was the last to go, burning to the ground in 1911. Now the dam is gone too. A lot of history slides by as you glide downstream, enjoying the laconic, meandering waterway.

The first things you slide by are the cranberry plants that dot both sides of the stream, plants that once provided a thriving commercial cranberry business. When you get to the camp downstream on your left, you won't realize that it was built to process those cranberries. As your eyes wander to admire the wetlands and forests on both sides of the stream, you won't imagine the open farm fields that once bordered the stream all the way to West Mount Vernon.

You'd have to get out into the woods, and see the barbed wire still clinging to old fence posts, to get a glimmer of just what that landscape looked like, back in the days when more

than half of Mount Vernon's 25,000 acres was cleared farmland. Today, less than 700 acres of open farmland remain.

Gaze to your left and imagine a time before the Revolution-
ary War when a group of loggers from Lewiston camped on
the hill, the highest spot in Mount Vernon. One man climbed
a tall tree to scout for those huge "King's" pines that were used
for ship masts. The climber was a man named Bowen, and the
hill still bears his name today. Two of the town's first families
established farms on Bowen Hill, raising mostly corn where
you now see nothing but trees.

When you get to "Three Rocks," you just passed, on the
left, the camping place of a small group of Penobscot Indians
who spent time there each year, making baskets from nearby
ash trees and sweetgrass.

Listen carefully and perhaps you'll hear the cries of glee of
the group of Campfire Girls, including Ruby Robinson, who
followed a blazed trail along the west side of the stream to the
Indian encampment so many years ago.

The Indians "pounded a section of ash log, still full of sap,
until the annual growth layers separated, and these they used
for making baskets," related Ruby. "With their guidance, each
of us made a small basket to take home. The Indians took
us back up the stream in their big canoes, standing tall and
straight as they paddled." They probably stood taller and
straighter than you do paddling your canoe downstream.

Here's something else to look for. In the lower section of
stream you will find a boulder with someone's initials carved
into it. Find out whose initials they are, and why they are
there. Nearby, you'll notice a pyramid of rocks underwater.
Figure out what critter made the pile, and why.

You may see a nesting loon burrowed into the reeds, halfway along on your trip, or a trio of deer swimming across in front of you. Perhaps our resident great horned owl will be settled high above the stream in his usual spot, or one of our great blue herons will burst from the grass beside you.

If it's November, you will surely spot me, hunting deer from my canoe. One year, I shot a 200-pound buck, just before sunset, and by the time I got it into the canoe and paddled back home, it was pitch black.

As I approached the bridge, my wife Linda and five-year-old son Joshua were on the bridge, watching for me. Lin shined her flashlight into the canoe and Josh spotted that big buck.

"Great fishing, Dad!" he exclaimed.

Hopkins Stream carries many stories in its slow current. Make some of them yours.

—*Overheard on the Way to Town*, Mount Vernon, 2010

Trashing My Woodlot

Could you blame me for posting NO TRESPASSING signs on
my Mount Vernon woodlot? Walk with me now on a beautiful sunny Saturday afternoon as we pick up the trash that
thoughtless, law-breaking slobs tossed onto my woodlot and
the adjoining land of my neighbors.

First into the trash bag is a large plastic bottle of Mountain
Dew—half full. Did you know it takes 450 years for a plastic
bottle to decompose? I picked up a lot of them, and can report
that trash-tossing idiots drink a great deal of low-fat milk.

A few steps further and we find the first of ten Bud Light
cans. We'll also pick up Bud Light bottles and cardboard containers. Bud Light rules the rural highways these days. As an
enthusiast of Maine's microbrews, I am proud to report that
I didn't find a single bottle or can for a Maine-made beer—
although I did find a copy of the August/September issue of
Brewing News. I paused beside the road to read it.

Next into the trash bag is a rusted highway marker with
a red flag attached, a golf ball, and a huge amount of shrink
wrap, followed soon after by our first coffee cup. Today's
pickup confirms that coffee drinkers prefer Dunkin', but most
of the area's purveyors of the dark liquid are represented. It is
apparent that the fast food and drinks purchased in Augusta
run out just when people get to Mount Vernon, and out the
window go the containers and bags.

Now we've found the first of many cigarette packs—Marl-
boro being the preference of drive-by litterers. And here we've
got a black hiking shoe, in good shape. I toss it into the bag

even though I know if I'd left it, the shoe would have decomposed in about eighty years.

Did I tell you I'm writing all of this down? We'll have more than five pages of items before we're done.

Energy drinks are numerous—it takes a lot of energy to toss them out the window—along with wooden debris, plastic pieces galore—and hey, here's a Black Cat Ammo Clip container. Alas, the clip is gone. But nearby we find a plastic container of fish hooks, with four hooks still in the container. I keep those for my grandsons.

I get excited just for a moment when I find a bottle of Elmer's Wood Filler, nearly full and partly buried. But the filler has been exposed to the weather and is no longer any good.

The wording on a nearby McDonald's drink container really irritates me: HERE'S TO YOU. A TOAST TO YOUR WISDOM, CLEVER DRINK BUYER. YOU HAVE SELECTED A CLASSIC FOUNTAIN BEVERAGE, PRECISELY MIXED FOR MAXIMUM REFRESHMENT. I'M LOVIN' IT. Well, I'm not lovin' it—or the slob who tossed it here.

Suddenly I get an idea. I'll package up the waste from each Augusta fast-food restaurant, drive there, and spread the trash around in their yards. Well, I'd probably just get arrested. But no one will be arrested for dumping the trash from those restaurants on my land.

Instead, I take a close look at a McDonald's bag, on the side of which is a phone number and the question, "How are we doing?" I called them to tell them just how they're doing. But after a long rigmarole of recorded instructions and no chance to talk to a live person, I gave up.

Something shiny blinks at me, and I reach down to pick up what appears to be a plastic container for a condom—sans condom. The language is foreign, but the word SEX is there, along with a photo of a naked couple enjoying—ahem. (No, I did not linger over the photo.)

I pick up two tires, one still on the wheel, a spent shotgun shell, a flowerpot, a paper plate covered with slugs, duct tape, broken glass, and then spot two full bags of garbage, sitting down over the bank. They turn out to be full of decaying frozen food. I have to re-bag them because the food is oozing out.

And here's another plain paper bag with the message FILL IT WITH OLD NEWSPAPERS TO BE RECYCLED. Apparently this person can't read; he filled it with a plastic six-pack container and three empty Budweiser cans.

Hauling the trash homeward, I stopped to visit a neighbor who thanked me for cleaning up the roadside and then spotted a bit of trash in the weeds out by the road. It turned out to be an advertisement for North Country Environmental Services.

Where were they when I needed them?!

—Central Maine Newspapers (October 10, 2012)

Roughing It in Maine

The imperfections are obvious and numerous. On the porch, a gap between the screen door and frame allows pesky mosquitoes inside. Sections of the floor are rotting. The wooden folding chairs were purchased at a yard sale twenty years ago.

Inside, the living room seats no more than four or five people comfortably, with three old rocking chairs and a very old couch. It's a pullout couch—*pullout* indicating the possibility it can be turned into an uncomfortable bed. It's too big to pull out of the building, or we'd probably have replaced it.

Lin put a new cover on the couch and cushions, proving that even the oldest, ugliest thing can be made handsome with a new cover—good news for me, as I get old and decrepit.

The two small bedrooms don't even accommodate our small family, never mind visitors. The springs on the twin beds in the kids' room give lumpy mattresses a good name.

Pink gleams through the gray floor in many places, giving us sort of a historical perspective on what was. The door and windows swell, meaning, sometimes they open and close and sometimes they don't.

The cane seats in two of the rockers are broken. Cushions keep us from falling through to the floor. The frame of my favorite photo—of twin fawns laying in the field behind us—is warped, but I haven't gotten around to reframing it.

I had to add small pieces of board to the bottom of the front door last year, to keep a troop of mice from visiting in the evening. Lin never warmed up to those visits, looking up from the couch to see a mouse skitter in under the door. It's amazing how they can squeeze through such a tiny gap—and be so fearsome when they get in.

Electric light fixtures—some with bulbs still in them—remind us of times past. The building was completely converted to propane thirteen years ago. Guess I could use the lightbulbs someplace else.

A long crack in the middle window pane over the kitchen sink is covered in duct tape. I broke the window four years ago. Two years ago I purchased a new pane—but, due to my faulty measurements, it was a quarter-inch too big. That's as close as I've gotten to fixing it. I find the duct tape decorative.

Speaking of the kitchen, it's so narrow that two people can't work there together, and the lack of cupboards leaves most food and supplies stocked on open shelves. At least you can see at a glance what you've got to eat.

Then there's the bathroom. The toilet sits on a piece of wood attached to the floor, leaving us precariously seated high above the floor, giving new meaning to the word *throne.* And the toilet is not anchored well, so the entire experience is a moving one. It's quite a ride.

The bathroom cupboard fell once and hit Hilary in the head. I nailed it back up on the wall, but everyone opens it with a bit of trepidation. So far, so good. There are no closets—and I mean, none at all. So the place has a cluttered look, with clothes and other stuff stored along walls and behind chairs.

Most of the plumbing is old, resulting in drips that are loud enough to keep you awake at night. We just replaced the kitchen faucet because I couldn't stand the steady drip, drip, drip any longer. The old faucets were rusted so tight I couldn't remove them to replace the washers.

Every spring, the building moves with the frost, giving us warped ceilings, jammed windows, and separated plumbing pipes. The weather here is brutal, so I have to paint the outside about every three years. Right now, the trim needs to be painted, along with the outside steps and deck. Maybe next year.

Two of our four lawn chairs are so rotten they're dangerous, and last week when Lin and I lifted the picnic table, the top came right off. The chairs and table all need paint and a sign stating SIT AT YOUR OWN RISK.

Moss grows on the porch roof, and I'm wondering if there's enough soil up there to plant some vegetables. Deer and other wildlife are so abundant that anything planted in the ground gets eaten as soon as it sprouts.

Last month Josh was seated on the deck at about eleven P.M. when a coyote came by, hunting the rabbits that live under our building. We share this building with bunnies, field mice, and red squirrels, and black ducks and geese wander around on the front lawn, begging for handouts. It's a veritable wild kingdom here. Yes, this place has a lot of imperfections. But it's camp. And it's perfect.

—*Kennebec Journal* (August 20, 2003)

. Update: Turns out it wasn't so perfect. Lin insists that I tell you we have new bedsprings and mattresses in the second bedroom, four spiffy L.L. Bean Adirondack chairs on the porch and deck, and the kids got us a very nice, new living-room couch. The kitchen window still sports duct tape. And the camp is still perfect.

The Signs of Country Life

Here's how to tell if you're living in the country:

- You're out before sunrise and the lights are on in the neighbor's home, and not for security.
- Droppings on the side of the road are from deer, turkeys, and other wild critters, not dogs and cats.
- The birdbath on the front lawn is an old bathtub.
- The best entertainment in town is the kids' ball game.
- The most powerful political group in town is the fire department.
- If the local country store doesn't have it, you don't need it.
- There is no mall and no fast-food restaurant.
- Your favorite department store is Renys, not Wal-Mart.
- You see more deer and turkeys than people.
- Some of the town's roads are gravel and closed in the winter.
- The good people have more guns than the criminals.
- When the woods are suddenly alive with the sound of gunfire, you don't call the police because you know it is the opening day of the deer season.
- You have a complete wardrobe of orange clothing and you wear it year-round.
- You wear camo clothing to hunt, not as a fashion statement.
- You wake up to the scent of lilacs, not the smell of car exhaust or factory fumes.

- The silence is filled with the songs of birds, not the wail of sirens.
- You see people carrying guns—and they're not the police.
- You see people carrying guns—and you're not afraid.
- You heat your house with wood that you cut on your own woodlot.
- When a car goes by your house, it is an event.
- Your ten-mile commute to work takes fifteen minutes, not an hour and a half.
- Neighbors passing in a vehicle on the road give you a wave.
- People you see at the store say hi, rather than look the other way.
- The trees you see have grown naturally and were not planted using money from a federal grant.
- You eat supper in the evening, not dinner. You never eat dinner.
- Your favorite restaurant is a church, and your favorite meal is a bean suppah.
- Your favorite perfume is Ben's 100.
- You can distinguish between midges, blackflies, mosquitoes, deerflies, moose flies, wood ticks, and deer ticks. You have become an expert in removing the latter after they take root in your skin.
- You know how to reduce the population of red squirrels and other varmints without using a Havahart trap.
- You make your own jams, jellies, pickles, and maple syrup.
- You share venison, pickles, jam, and more with your neighbors.

- You are not offended by the smell of manure on a farmer's field (or dropped on the road from his tractor while it travels between fields).
- Instead of wrought-iron or wood fencing, you put up electric.
- When you see a white-tailed deer, you think of steaks, not Bambi.
- You get excited when you see a bear, not scared.
- You see more bald eagles than pigeons.
- Your idea of a night out is sitting on the front porch in your rocking chair.
- Nonresidents pay more than 50 percent of your town's property taxes.
- You still call the transfer station the dump.
- You bring more stuff home from the dump than you deliver there.
- You get most of your news at the local café.
- You have a root cellar.
- You have enough canned food in the root cellar to survive any national emergency.
- You make do, and you know what that means.
- You eat breakfast, never brunch.
- You can see the stars, and the northern lights are not just something you've heard about.
- You know all the people you see in town.
- A fishing trip is a thirty-second stroll to the water, not a two-hour drive.
- Your boat doesn't sail.
- The only time you see an out-of-state license plate is in July and August, and you see a lot of them then.

- Your favorite magazine is *Uncle Henry's.*
- You paint the front of your house and let the back go.
- You don't need a building permit for an outhouse, tree house, or doghouse.
- You don't have a town manager. You do have selectmen, and many of them are women.
- You understand that trees grow back after they are cut down.
- You know the difference between a hardwood and a softwood.
- You realize that fiddleheading has nothing to do with fiddles.
- You can fix things, but don't until it's an emergency.
- You don't need a permit to have a lawn sale.
- A flag flies in your front yard.
- City people secretly envy you.

'Fess up; you know you do.

—Central Maine Newspapers (June 26, 2013)

Mexico Memoir Is a Must-Read

Two years ago I met Monica Wood in Portland's Western Cemetery, home to the Longfellow family tomb. We were both bird-watching. I was thrilled to meet one of my favorite novelists and tell her how much I enjoyed all four of her novels.

Of course, I inquired as to when I could expect novel number five, and was disappointed to hear that instead of a novel, she was working on a memoir of growing up in Mexico, Maine. I couldn't imagine a memoir about this Maine mill town that would be as compelling as one of Monica's novels. Or even interesting.

Wow, was I ever wrong! A few weeks ago I received *When We Were the Kennedys*, Monica Wood's extraordinary, powerful, and moving memoir of her close, Irish Catholic immigrant family of father, mother, son, and four daughters.

Monica's dad dropped dead on his way to work at the Oxford Paper Company, or, as they called it, "The Oxford," the mill that dominated Rumford and Mexico as the principal employer in the 1960s. Monica was nine years old. And this is where her memoir begins.

This heart-wrenching, emotional, sometimes funny, oftentimes astonishing, and always compelling story is far better than the best novel—and not just because it's a true story. It is a powerful story, one that may be familiar to those who grew up in one-mill Maine towns, but not as well known to the rest of us.

You will find yourself pausing, rereading entire paragraphs, and thinking about what you've read—perhaps stirring memories of your own Mexico.

Three years after Monica's dad died, I would ride into Mexico on a school bus as a member of my Winthrop High School basketball team, to play in Mexico's tiny gym, so small that the circles on the floor overlapped. It was our last game of the season, and we arrived undefeated and cocky. The Mexico team featured a couple of very short, stocky, and quick guards, and they beat us.

It was a stinging defeat, but even more memorable to me was the sulfur stench of the town, the grittiness, the huge dominating presence of the Oxford Paper Company. I was very glad to get out of town.

Monica captures the heart and soul of a Maine mill town—and a time that is long gone. Today, Monica notes, "The sign across the river says NewPage, after the investment company that bought out MeadWestvaco, which bought out Mead, which bought out Boise Cascade, which bought out Ethyl, which bought out The Oxford." I might add that the three thousand jobs at The Oxford in the 1960s have shrunk to 750 today at NewPage, a company that is in bankruptcy.

This memoir could be taken as a fond farewell to Maine's once-thriving small towns, but it is a lot more than that. I see it as a lovingly told tale expressed with remarkable insights but without judgment.

In Monica's words, her memoir is a chance "to look back, with new eyes, on what you did not know you knew." It's hard to accept that I came to and left Mexico and never knew anything of this remarkable story. With this memoir, Monica has allowed me to look back on Mexico with new eyes, and learn what I did not know in 1966. She must have shed a lot of tears writing this book, as I did reading it.

I won't even try to describe the heartbreaking yet somehow uplifting troubles of this dad-less family living in a desperate Maine mill town. But I should note, given the title, that President Kennedy's assassination—the same year her dad died—plays an important part in bringing understanding to young Monica.

Following the loss of her dad, Monica retreated into books: "I'd always loved books for their reassuring heft, for their promise of new words, for their air of mystery, for the characters who lived in them, for the sublime pleasure of disappearing."

After many years of perhaps disappearing into her own novels, in this memoir, Monica reappears, ensuring that even though The Oxford, Mexico High School, and even Monica herself are gone from that small mill town on the east side of the Androscoggin River, this place will never be forgotten.

—Central Maine Newspapers (July 25, 2012)

Good-bye to Carleton Woolen Mill

Carleton Woolen Mill in Winthrop put me through college, but not in the way you might think. I worked one summer in the mill, mostly on the night shift, and the work was so hard that it propelled me on to college, knowing that I didn't want to spend my life in the mill.

Sometime during that hot summer, with itchy wool stuck to my sweaty back, I figured out that a college education was mighty important.

On Saturday, Winthrop celebrates Carleton Woolen Mill Workers' Appreciation Day with a celebration from ten A.M. to two P.M. at the Winthrop Middle School. The public as well as former mill workers are invited.

Of course, all Carleton workers are former, because the mill closed for good in the spring of 2000, when more than 300 workers lost their jobs. After almost 188 years of manufacturing woolens in Winthrop, Carleton went belly up because of a declining world market and foreign competition.

"We hope the whole town will show up to tell these folks how much we appreciate everything they did," said Chris McEwan, the event's coordinator.

So do I. If the mill workers turn out, there will be some real characters there. I was astonished to learn that one of those characters is my friend Gary Crocker, the Maine humorist who got his first job at Carleton Woolen Mill. No wonder he has such a great sense of humor.

Gary will display some of that humor at Saturday's festivities, and I hope he has some good stories of fun times down in

31

the bowels of the mill where the sun doesn't shine, and where huge eels provided a lot of entertainment for me and my fishing buddies.

No, I didn't fish during my shift. But when I wasn't working, the millstream that flowed right under the Main Street mill provided fast fishing action.

The day before Winthrop's celebration, all of Maine's woolen workers will be honored at Maine Woolen Worker Day at the State House. Those of us who toiled in woolen mills throughout the state will be honored for our efforts and contributions to the state's economy.

My own efforts and contributions were somewhat limited. I did work my way up from toting heavy bales of woolen cloth to driving a forklift. In fact, I experienced practically all of the jobs in the mill that summer. They even set me to stitching the cloth together for a while alongside a brigade of ladies. I really did like that job.

The job I loathed was cleaning the acid baths that the cloth was run through. I remember the job included pure ammonia, and didn't that sting the old eyes!

But the job didn't require my full attention, and one early morning I was sleeping on a pile of cloth near my machinery when the owner, Mr. Goldfine, walked through. At least, that was what I was told. I never actually woke up to see him go by. But I wasn't fired either, so I kept showing up for work, punching the time clock day after day after day.

The noise when all of those machines were running was deafening. And of course, we didn't have much in the way of safety equipment then. I was probably lucky to emerge with my hearing intact and all my limbs still attached. But of course, I only toiled there for one summer.

The next summer I went into banking. Yeah, that was more like it. My job at the bank was like a vacation compared to working in the mill. So I never looked back.

This Friday and Saturday I will look back to honor those fine folks, including my wife's dad, who stuck it out, day after day, month after month, year after year. Because I know in my heart I never would have been able to do that.

But for one summer, those folks were my best friends. I worked beside them, listened to their stories, knew their hopes and dreams, shared their tedious and difficult jobs—and left the mill at the end of that summer more mature, more fit, and more determined to get on with my life.

For all of that, I thank each and every one of them.

—*Kennebec Journal* (May 16, 2001)

Down East **Magazine Reveals Secret**

Down East magazine has ruined my summer.

FIFTEEN SMALL-TOWN GETAWAYS was the colorful front-page headline in *Down East's* April edition. I ripped the magazine open to page 76 to see the list of getaway towns and nearly fell to the floor. The world went dark.

My town of Mount Vernon has been discovered.

Down East encouraged visitors to "Step Out in Stonington, Bird-Watch in Jonesport, Go Yachting in York Harbor, Get Historical in Fort Kent, Rough It in Kakadjo," and, to my great dismay, "Take it Slow in Mount Vernon."

I could not believe what I was reading in this Camden-based magazine, heretofore one of my favorites. After mentioning the thousands of summer tourists that flock to the Belgrade lakes, it reported that they often miss Mount Vernon, a small town without crowds, nestled against Flying Pond and Parker Pond. Sure, we didn't have crowds—until *Down East* spilled the beans.

The magazine article revealed details about Shop at the Corner and Lakeside Serendipity, two stores in the village that sell unique, Maine-made products and collectibles, respectively. If the kids get bored with the "relaxing pace of this quaint village," *Down East* recommended a trip to DEW Animal Kingdom and Sanctuary, an exotic animal farm. May you get eaten by a lion! And we are not quaint!

I will prove it by looking up the definition. My dictionary defines *quaint* as—uh-oh, maybe they got this right—"strikingly old-fashioned" or "unusual or different in character." Guilty as charged! We're quaint, and ain't we some proud of it!

The magazine article also exposed the Lakeside Loft, "a charming bed-and-breakfast right on the shore of Minnehonk Lake that provides canoes and kayaks for guests," and The Olde Post Office Café, which can put up picnic supplies.

That does it! I won't be able to get a table anymore at Maine's best café. Oh, how I will miss those delectable sandwiches and pastries, and the best coffee in a hundred miles, and that Saturday-night live music, and . . . and . . . oh, I just can't stand it. And those kayaks and canoes will be traveling—by the hundreds, probably—across Minnehonk Lake and right down Hopkins Stream beside my house. Can someone tell me where to buy underwater explosives?

Dear former friends at *Down East* magazine: Cancel my subscription. And don't even think about coming to town. The café is packed. You can no longer get a room at the Loft. We never should have let Wayne and Christine turn Ray Neal's old garage into such a charming place.

And DEW's wild, ravenous beasts all got loose and are roaming the fields and forests. They're angry. And hungry.

Surely Camden has enough restaurants, gift shops, and quaintness to keep you folks busy all summer. We are familiar with your *Peyton Place* reputation. That ought to be enough to keep you home. Nothing like that happens in Mount Vernon. At least, we don't make a movie out of it.

When do the tourists start coming? I hear they come earlier every year—something to do with global warming. This is important. I need to head to camp before they arrive here.

If *Down East* ever mentions the northern Maine lake my camp is on, I will personally lead a brigade to take their tourist-loving headquarters in Camden and turn it into a wine bar—a quaint wine bar.

Wait a minute. Wait a minute. My eyes drift to the bottom of the front page of that *Down East* edition. Oh no! RANGELEY'S LEGENDARY LAKES—DISCOVER MAINE'S BEST FISHING trumpets the headline. It's a "special 12-page section."

Is nothing sacred? My beloved Kennebago River, just an hour from home, and a favorite fishing spot. Upper Dam. Lakewood Camps' charming and isolated lodge on the Rapid River, home to Maine's biggest wild brook trout. *Down East* names names. And gives directions!

Darn these people! Can't they catch enough mackerel and striped bass on the Camden coast? We don't need more tourist anglers on my favorite Rangeley waters.

Hold on. Another of the magazine's headlines grabs my attention: BALDACCI'S SECRET GARDEN. Aha! It's secret no more, governor! For inviting these nosy people from *Down East* into your garden, may the tourists trample your tasty tomatoes and take some of your precious peppers home as souvenirs.

The tourists are coming. I'm retreating to the North Woods. Have a great summer.

—Central Maine Newspapers (April 23, 2008)

A Camp Full of Memories

Our camp in Maine's North Woods on the shore of Sourdnahunk Lake is relaxing and restorative. And after twenty-two
wonderful years there, it's now a camp full of memories.

My mom and dad visited us at camp each summer, and we
surprised them there with a celebration of their fiftieth wedding
anniversary. They didn't know we'd invited my brother's and
sister's families until they started arriving. It was an anniversary
none of us will ever forget, including the hymn sing.

Dad had never fly-fished, and Sourdnahunk is fly-fishing
only, so he gave it a try. While he never mastered the art of
casting, he could get his fly out there far enough to catch fish.
He took the boat out early one morning and came back just
as Mom, Lin, and I were getting up. I knew from the look on
Dad's face as he pushed open the screen door that he'd caught
a fish. And what a fish it was! A gorgeous, fat, colorful, fifteen-
and-a-half-inch brook trout—the biggest we'd catch that
entire season. One reason I'll never forget it is that Dad carved
a copy of that fish and it's hanging on a wall at camp.

After Mom died, Dad started coming up with me to open
camp each spring. He's ninety years old now and doesn't travel
far from home, but I will never forget those trips.

Our kids grew up here. I took Rebekah, Josh, and Hilary
on a backcountry camping trip one August into Wassataquoik
Lake. Because it was August, I told them it would be warm and
we would not need sleeping bags. I carried a couple of blankets with us, along with pots and pans and food. Little Hilary

insisted on her tiny sleeping bag, so she carried it the entire five miles attached to her backpack.

It came in handy. The nights were freezing! In our lean-to, I unzipped Hil's sleeping bag and used it to cover all three kids. None of us got much sleep. But I can still see the kids prancing in falling water at the stunningly beautiful Green Falls. And the memories of that trip do get better over time.

My wife Linda, Josh, and Hilary all learned to fly-fish here. Linda would occasionally accompany me in the boat for an evening of fishing, but she'd sit and read while I fished—until the fishing really heated up. One time I had been casting for an hour with little luck. Lin sensed that it was time to try it. She picked up her rod, made one cast, and landed a thirteen-and-a-half-inch trout. She smiled and sat back down to read some more. She always caught the biggest trout of the evening. It was a humbling experience, and a memory for me.

I tried unsuccessfully to teach Josh to cast, so you can imagine how much fun it is today to sit in the boat and watch him cast so beautifully and flawlessly. How'd he learn to do that? He casts a lot better than me now. And every evening we're out on the water, I put more memories in the bank.

Josh also became my go-to fly tier. He ties the Sourdnahunk Yarn Fly, something a friend taught him to tie years ago. It's the only fly we use to fish the lake's famous green drake hatch. Fortunately, Josh is still tying those for me.

Some of my best memories of fishing involve Hilary. I see her at five years of age, sitting on a downed tree across a small brook, holding her alder twig and string with a hook and worm on it, hauling tiny trout out of the water and squealing with glee. That alder rod is still hanging on the porch. Yes, you can hang on to some memories by hanging them up!

Hilary also learned to tie flies, but hers were always her own colorful creations. I've got a wonderful photo of Hil in Sourdnahunk Stream, holding up a very small brook trout, the first fish she ever caught on her own fly. I had carried her on my back across the stream, where she was able to reach a small pool of fish. She caught a bunch of fish, but that first one is the one we'll both never forget.

My sister Edie and her boys, Nate and Ezra, have also contributed to my camp memories. One year they were up visiting us when Nate said he had never seen a moose and really, really wanted to see one. That evening I took them out into the bog behind camp, where we stood behind a bush near the water. Ten minutes later a large cow moose walked right by us, just ten yards away. To this day, Nate thinks I am a fantastic guide! Little does he know how much luck played in that particular memory.

These days Rebekah is creating memories with her visits to camp with husband Patrick and our grandsons Vishal and Addison. Lin and I get up here with them when we can, although often we like to let them have their own special time here.

Labor Day weekend of 2012, I forded Sourdnahunk Stream with five-year-old Vishal on my back. Then I placed him on the ground and we hiked a few hundred yards to one of my favorite pools, hoping to catch some native brook trout.

Because he hadn't yet learned to cast flies, I did the casting, then handed the fly rod to Vishal. He immediately began reeling, hooked the fish, and hauled them in. We both whooped it up. There are no sweeter words than "I've got another one, Grampy!"

I took the hooks out of the trout, handed them to V, and he carefully released them back into the stream. We caught twenty-four trout in an hour and a half of the most fun you can have with a grandchild.

Trout number twenty-one was a whopper. As soon as Vishal released the fish, I made another cast, only to hear him exuberantly exclaim, "Grampy, we're both very happy!" Boy, he got that right!

There are memories of climbing Baxter Park's mountains with the kids. There's that time that Josh almost drowned at Ledge Falls—not really, but that's how he remembers it! There was the famous whiffle ball game in the backyard where a doe deer came out and sniffed the whiffle ball, apparently thinking it was a salt lick. The time we were all walking the driveway when a big black bear ambled down the road toward us, went into the woods to walk around us, and then came out in the driveway just below us.

I've got photos of Josh chasing a ten-point buck up over the lawn and Lin feeding a tame fox. Wildlife memories abound. We saw so many moose at camp that when Lin or I would exclaim, "There's a moose on the lawn," Hilary would not even look up from her book!

Lin and I now travel to camp alone most of the time, relishing our memories there while making new ones. Yesterday she saw her first pine marten. It almost ran her over on the road as we were out bird-watching. Memories at camp just keep on coming.

Battling Wildlife in the Home

Running a bit late for a selectmen's meeting one evening years ago, I dashed down the stairs into my workshop without turning on the light. Approaching the door to the garage, I felt our cat move across my feet in front of me and reached down to pet him. Bad mistake.

The skunk blasted me right in the face. I staggered, and started running back upstairs, shedding my stinking clothing along the way before jumping into the shower. Linda later collected the clothing and threw it away.

Eventually I got to the selectmen's meeting. No one sat near me.

Last week I wrote about Jim Sterba's book, *Nature Wars;* it offers a fascinating look at out-of-control populations of wildlife, explains why this has happened, and relates many backyard battles with a variety of critters from deer to beaver. Sterba neglected one crucial aspect of this problem: when the battles move into the home.

And I'm not just talking about mice, although we've done battle with plenty of them. One winter I caught thirty-eight, an even dozen of them trapped in a kitchen drawer. And this doesn't count the mice our cat killed. Often we wake in the middle of the night to a commotion in the dining room outside our bedroom door, as the cat and his quarry careen around the room. Sometimes I have to get up and stomp the mouse to death. My stomping record is eight, in a two-week period.

Bats are a particular challenge. In the early years, I'd try to kill them with a fireplace poker. For years there was a hole in our kitchen ceiling where I once missed a bat with the poker. Since getting educated to the benefits bats bring to the neighborhood, and worried about their diminishing populations, I now catch them in a long-handled fishing net, gently releasing them outside.

Then there was the snake episode.

Linda hates snakes. One day as she was washing the kitchen floor, she moved a wicker basket that I'd left outside for some time the day before, and a large snake slithered out of the bottom of the basket.

She grabbed the fireplace shovel and jumped up on a kitchen chair, gradually bludgeoning the harmless thing to death. At one point in this fierce battle, she called me on the phone. All I could do was encourage her to keep at it. She was still shook up when I got home, and always shudders when I bring up the incident.

Every wild critter that can get into the house, does so. Red squirrels are particularly nettlesome. I watch for them at the bird feeder, and if they turn toward the house after dining, I shoot them. If they head for the woods, they get a reprieve. A chipmunk currently resides in my workshop and the garage, darting into a tunnel under the cement floor when he sees me.

One sunny Saturday morning, I opened the bulkhead door to air out the cellar. A bit later, heading out of the cellar up the bulkhead's steps, I met a huge raccoon coming down the steps. We had a stare-down, and he eventually reversed course. I'm not sure what would have happened if he'd continued down the steps. He was certainly too big to stomp to death.

And then there is the night I woke to a terrible ruckus directly below my pillow, under the floor. Turned out to be mating raccoons.

One morning Lin was getting ready for school and there was a chickadee on her computer, apparently brought into the house by the cat. Another time, the cat brought in a sparrow. Lin yelled at the cat and he dropped the bird. It promptly lifted off and flew into my office. Lin put on a pair of gloves and chased the bird around the room, finally catching and setting it outside. Not all wildlife-in-the-home stories have a bad ending.

But some of these encounters are frightening, especially the rabid fox that entered our garage while I was out of town. Lin called the local game warden and he came and shot it. Our dog, chained in the front yard, had to be quarantined for a while, even though we weren't sure it ever got near the fox. All was well that ended well.

And I guess that's the message here: Choosing to live in and around their homes, we must expect, occasionally, that these wild critters will like our homes. Some we can live with. Some, not so much.

—Central Maine Newspapers (2013)

Protecting Rural Character

The most popular places to live in the 1980s in Kennebec County were Wayne, Litchfield, and Mount Vernon, in that order. Wayne's population increased by an astonishing 51 percent during the decade, while Litchfield was attracting 35 percent more people, and Mount Vernon, 33 percent.

The misconception of the decade was that Manchester, Readfield, and Winthrop were the best and most attractive places to locate a new home. Manchester grew just 7.7 percent, Readfield, only 4.6 percent, and Winthrop barely held its own, with 1.3 percent growth. I guess they never replaced Linda and me when we moved from Winthrop to Mount Vernon in 1979.

Clearly our smaller, rural communities have something people seek. It might be called rural character. Today Maine's Growth Management Act challenges us to protect the rural character of our communities, direct growth to appropriate areas, and conserve our natural resources. Many towns are struggling to meet this new state mandate.

What, for example, does "rural character" consist of? Why is it that Wayne, Litchfield, and Mount Vernon seem to have more of it than Manchester, Readfield, and Winthrop? How do we protect it without ruining it?

The term *rural* conjures up images of a visual landscape of farms, stone walls, winding, tree-lined roads running up and down hillsides, and a diversity of architecture and people. Important rural characteristics include a lot of open space and forest, abundant wildlife, clean water, large homesteads, and a diverse development pattern with homes spread throughout the land base. In many communities the lack of cluttered and clustered development is a special rural characteristic.

To some the term *rural* represents an attitude: independence, freedom, and neighborliness in an environment where you know you can trust your neighbors. Doors are left unlocked, keys left in cars. When problems occur, neighbors resolve them by talking with each other.

Residents of rural areas also value the opportunity to be left alone. As the late Bill Clark wrote in his story, "Ridge Runner's Lament" (part of the book *The Hills of Maine*), "It is crowded here. The houses are close. The hammers pound every day and bring the houses closer. The area boosters look for more people, more people, more people. People are progress. People are prosperity. People are wonderful.

"That's all right," wrote Bill. "I can stand people. But I don't like their permanent presence in planned proximity. I like to be with them and then I like to be alone. When I'm alone, I don't want to know that there is a house fifty feet away in which lives another man who also wants to be alone."

There is more self-sufficiency (although much less than in the past) in rural areas—people can take care of their own. When the electricity goes off, rural people don't panic. Many believe that an important rural characteristic is the lack of regulations and allowance for creativity and diversity, which gives even the poorest people an opportunity to house themselves.

Rural can also be defined as what it is not. No noise, no public services, no regulations, no streetlights, no violent crime.

Rural is a place where people live from the land, not just on the land. Land is a sustaining factor of life in rural Maine. Use of the land is an essential characteristic of rural life, and rural people live closer to their land and natural resources. *Rural* means the chance to sell a few cords of wood off the back forty, to hunt behind the house, and to see deer all over town. *Rural* is church on Sunday and the country store all week long.

Rural is the place where outdoor recreation prevails over indoor sports, where maple syrup is boiled in the spring from maple ridges where snowmobiles and snowshoers abound in winter. It's a place where summer vacationers leave before the spectacular beauty of the fall returns Maine to its natives.

A diversity of land, homes, and people make up the character which we regard today as rural. Can it be saved?

Winthrop was a rural town when I grew up there. I sold my 4-H vegetables on Main Street in front of Dad's store, and knew every customer. Today neither Dad's store nor my 4-H club is there. I walked a mile to a school complex that housed every grade, kindergarten to high school. I knew every kid in town, and played with most of them. Today, schools are spread out, and kids who live within sight of the school ride the bus.

I hiked and hunted the hills, trapped along the streams, fished along the shoreline, swam from the uncrowded beach. Today the beach is wall-to-wall people, the lakes are fully developed, the hills have sprouted houses, most of the land is posted, and any trapper would catch more cats than muskrats.

This doesn't mean Winthrop is not a beautiful and wonderful place to live; it's just not rural anymore. Mount Vernon and Wayne and Litchfield are rural. We'll need all the creativity we can muster to keep them that way.

—*Kennebec Journal* (February 11, 1991); my first weekly column, after writing an occasional op-ed column for two years

Dad's Last Barn Sale—Maybe

Last year he promised it would be his last. No more barn sales. He was cleaned out.

He was not truthful. He was not cleaned out. Worse, Dad has continued to gather stuff from the yard sales of others, from the town dump, from *Uncle Henry's* cornucopia of used goods.

In the past year he started to buy in bulk: 40 pairs of snow-shoes, 150 model lobster boats. It is frightening. So at eight A.M., Saturday, Ezra Smith's famous annual barn sale on Lambert Street in Winthrop will be held again—and let me predict now that it will not be the last, despite the pleadings of all of his children.

A barn sale is a step up from the yard sale, promising old things that have been stored in a barn loft for too many years. In Dad's case, it is a house, barn, garage, shed, and outbuildings sale. Each location is stuffed with the old, unique, secondhand, and just plain used items that Dad has gathered for the elite shoppers who line up at the end of his driveway, starting at six-thirty in the morning, chanting his name and demanding that he open up his famous sale.

No one gets in early. So if you show up at eight, that will be okay. Actually, you can show up in the last five minutes, at 1:55 P.M., and still find an amazing collection of—sorry, Dad—junk. I know, one man's junk is another man's treasure, and over the years, a lot of treasure has gone down that driveway in the hands of someone who either found it useful or enchanting.

47

Even me. Yes, I am one of Dad's best customers, although my record of payment is not all that strong. I have gotten Adirondack chairs, golf clubs, baskets, kid's toys, a chest of drawers, tools, hatchets, gardening supplies, the world's best can opener (no exaggeration), a gorgeous blue bowl, and doughnuts—the only things certain to be fresh that day, because sister Edie brings them.

This year, the offerings include two canoes with paddles, a snowblower, a mind-boggling array of old tools, probably some of my old political buttons and posters, and yes, oh, yes, enough lobster buoys to start your own business. Also available are plenty of lamps and baskets, and the antique washing machine is a classic, not to be passed up. There are framed prints, paintings, picture frames, lumber, a very interesting collection of miniature pheasants, and plenty of furniture (including four coffee tables)—plus a parcel of vacuum cleaners to keep that furniture nice and spiffy.

The old baby carriage is worth a look. If you could help reduce his collection of golf clubs, we would be mighty appreciative. And please take home a pair of snowshoes.

There is always a pile of free stuff. Don't miss that.

Dad does have some standards. There are no clothes, although my wife would love to offer up some of my best apparel. And I am sorry to report that the moose antlers are gone—but there are plenty of deer antlers. And the fish and birds that Dad carves are always for sale.

The Smith clan arrives at the crack of dawn to mine through the sheds and outbuildings and barn loft, pulling the treasures out to the driveway and yard for display. I have forgotten how many years we have done this. Let's see; I am fifty-seven. Seems like I must have been doing this for about seventy years.

It is only discouraging when I pull out the same stuff I pulled out the previous year, knowing that these perennial items will remain once again after all the good stuff is gone. Then we have to put them back. But once in a while, Dad will ship a truckload to an auction house, so he does have other methods of paring down the collection.

If he would only stop going to the Winthrop transfer station, we might get ahead of the stuff. I am certain when they changed the name from town dump to town transfer station, they did not mean transfer your junk to Ezra Smith. The stuff is supposed to go to a landfill, not to Lambert Street.

Going to the dump empty and coming home full is something Dad must have patented. In fact, if he has brought some of your stuff home from the dump, you have an obligation to come get it on Saturday morning. No questions asked. The price will be right.

You will see his signs out on Route 202 and all over town, and they will lead you right to the junkyard—excuse me— barn sale. Be there. Please. And don't go home empty-handed.

—Central Maine Newspapers (July 20, 2005)

Update: After this was published, a letter writer complained that I used the column to promote Dad's barn sale. Guilty as charged! And Dad is still having barn sales.

Plates Need a Little License

As we move into summer, which officially begins today in Maine, needing something to talk about besides the weather and tourists, legislators have come through by opening debate on a new license plate.

An eleven-member panel chaired by Representative William O'Gara (D-Westbrook) is working this summer to come up with a new plate design that would be available by July 1, 1999. O'Gara says he's not a great fan of the generic lobster plate. He likes the loon plate.

My first reaction is to leave the red crustacean alone. It helps sell loon plates. Some folks would pay anything to avoid having that awful red bug on their plates.

If we make the new generic plate too attractive, some may give up their loon plates, which cost $20 extra and provide dedicated revenue for state parks and endangered species programs. Maine sponsors the most popular conservation license plate program in the country, and the lobster plate is our secret weapon.

Recognizing that a new plate is inevitable, however, let's use some imagination. In Dan McGillvray's *Kennebec Journal* article, Angela Harrington of Augusta's Gilbert School suggested a furry woods animal. She'd like the snowshoe hare.

Fifth-grade classmates suggested a beaver, coyote, pinecone and tassel, and a mosquito. Other kids chimed in with a black bear, deer, and eagle. Alex Poulin favors the state bird, the chickadee-dee-dee.

I favor the blackfly. Let's be brutally honest: The front plate should feature dozens of blackflies, printed at random all over the plate. Then when the real things get squashed on the plate, they'll blend right in.

The back plate should feature the rear end of a moose. And all Maine vehicles should be issued a pair of small plastic moose antlers for hood ornaments. Ninety-five percent of the tourists I encounter in Maine are looking for a moose. Let's make it easy for them! In fact, we could sell the moose antler hood ornaments to tourists and make enough so our sets could be free.

Scent is important now in some products, and we could make our plates really distinctive by adding scent capsules that would gradually release the scent of a pine forest or salty coastal air.

Adapting the entire vehicle to the license plate concept, your horn could present the sound of the animal on your plate. The growl of a black bear might cause the slow-moving vehicle in front of you to pull right over and let you pass.

Daughter Hilary suggests a chickadee sitting on a pine tassel with a cone. Nope. Too nice. It would hurt the sale of loon plates.

Of course, you could take Hilary's concept a bit further: Print the entire plate so it appears to be a piece of gorgeous green tourmaline (Maine's state mineral). Use Hilary's chickadee (state bird) and pinecone and tassel (state flower), but include the entire pine tree (state tree), abuzz with honeybees (state insect). Along the bottom have Moosehead Lake (largest lake) at the foot of Mount Katahdin (tallest mountain), with a landlocked salmon (state fish) jumping out of the lake.

Finally, instead of those annual red or green registration stickers, let's put on stickers featuring our favorite politicians or products. We could be free to sell that space to the highest bidder and collect enough so our plates could be free. You could rent that space by the month. One month your plate could feature Renys; the next, Marden's.

The back plate offers even more room for imagination. I like the idea of featuring the back end of a favorite animal. Depending on our point of view, you might present the rear end of a skunk, tail up. Combine that with my idea for scent capsules, and you'd have no problem clearing out a parking lot and getting a space.

A favorite tavern in Washington, D.C., features the tail ends of a buck and doe deer over their respective restrooms. That offers interesting possibilities for our license plates.

Finally, we should get a slogan on our license plate that reflects our reality. VACATIONLAND is far too subservient. THE WAY LIFE SHOULD BE is too absurd. DIRIGO may be our state motto, but it's out-of-date. Perhaps something like WE'RE STILL HERE, or MORE TREES THAN PEOPLE. I kind of like GO SOX!

—*Kennebec Journal* (July 1, 1996)

Update: We got the chickadee with the pinecone and tassel, but also, after ten years of trying, sportsmen got a sportsman's plate featuring a moose and brook trout. All the other ideas are still pending.

The Renys Are a Rare Brand

Bob Reny loved to sell things at bargain prices, and he sure was good at it. He just didn't want to sell them on Sunday. Of all my memories of Bob, and I have many good ones, the most vivid is his hard-fought campaign to prevent large stores— including his own—from opening on Sundays. I was on the other side.

The congenial Reny, who died on July 24, 2009, at age eighty-three, opened his first store in Damariscotta in 1949, and grew the discount retail business to fourteen locations, selling clothing, hardware, sporting goods, food, and lots of specialty items—anything Bob could obtain and sell at a substantial discount.

Shoppers could never be sure what they'd find at Renys, but they knew it would be good, and they knew it would be cheap. Renys survives today by sticking to the strategies created by their founder: good products at good prices.

Many Mainers are very loyal to the store, and it's not unusual for an entire community to plead with the family to open a Renys in their town. Bob and his family—a rare brand—have been cautiously smart in their expansions, sticking to towns and locations where they can thrive by offering low-cost items that everyone needs and great customer service.

If Renys doesn't have it, you don't need it. My wife and I have sometimes looked unsuccessfully for items elsewhere and then surprised ourselves when we finally located the product at Renys in Farmington. Bob favored downtown locations, and was the rare small retailer who could compete against the megastores, from W. T. Grant and Zayre in the past to Kmart and Wal-Mart today.

My dad was one of Bob's competitors as an owner of Wilson's Dollar Stores, another chain of small five-and-dimes, but Dad never had anything but good words when we talked about Bob.

Celebrating its sixtieth anniversary this year, Renys Department Stores is one of Maine's longest-surviving family businesses. Today, two of Bob's three sons run the business.

Bob was a political activist, an outspoken Republican, and a leader of the Maine Merchants Association. He spent a lot of time advocating at the legislature for the state's retail industry. I was on his side in many political battles, and immensely enjoyed his energy, enthusiasm, honesty, commitment, values, and sense of humor. He was a very funny man.

But in 1990, Bob was not amused by the campaign to allow Sunday shopping. At that time, only stores with less than 5,000 square feet could open on Sundays. Larger stores and malls organized a citizens' initiative campaign so that all stores could open on Sunday. My sister and I managed the petition drive that qualified the initiative for the ballot, and later worked on the referendum campaign.

Bob strongly opposed the initiative, even though he could have made more money by opening on Sundays. He didn't want his employees to have to work on Sundays, and he knew if all the other stores opened that day, he'd have to open too. Our campaign was well funded by the big stores, while Bob's was run on a shoestring.

Today, many would be amazed that just nineteen years ago, we couldn't shop on Sundays at the mall and in the big stores. If anyone suggested today that all large stores close on Sundays, he'd be laughed out of the state. But Bob Reny was not laughing in 1990, and he single-handedly came close to defeating our initiative.

He predicted, accurately, that many small stores would go out of business because they got most of their revenue on Sundays when the big stores were not open. He pitched the rural Maine lifestyle, advocated for the small stores that needed Sunday shoppers, focused on the importance of Sunday's day of rest and relaxation for Maine families, and fought hard to protect Maine's uniqueness.

The campaign was interesting, informative, and life-changing for many Mainers. A total of 518,507 people voted on the referendum question on November 6, 1990. A surprisingly narrow majority, 52.7 percent, voted for Sunday shopping. But an amazing 47.5 percent voted to keep the stores closed on that day. Almost a quarter of a million voters didn't want the big stores to open for their shopping pleasure on Sundays.

Bob never held my work on that campaign against me, a true measure of the man, but he lamented to me, more than once, what a great mistake we had made. He may have been right.

He certainly will be missed.

—Central Maine Newspapers (August 19, 2009)

Russ Libby Was a Humble Man

From Mount Vernon to the nation's capital and far beyond, the accolades for Russ Libby, upon his untimely death, would only have embarrassed him. Russ was a humble man, never eager for the limelight, although he often deserved it.

Robert Shetterly's portrait of Russ for his series, *Americans Who Tell the Truth,* is profound, as is the quote from Russ that accompanies the portrait: "We have to challenge the idea that contamination is just the price of living in the modern world. Our bodies don't have systems to process plastics or flame retardants or pesticides. If contamination is the price of modern society, modern society has failed us."

Russ's body certainly wasn't able to fend off the chemical contamination. On July 16, 2012, in a Maine Compass column for this newspaper, Russ told his story. One of thirteen Maine participants in a study of chemical pollutants, Russ was astonished to find that his body had the most contaminants of all the participants, including fire retardants.

In that column, which should be reprinted at least once a year and widely distributed, Russ wrote, "I've had a lot of occasions to think about the study since then. Eighteen months ago, I was diagnosed with two different forms of cancer—kidney and prostate—and I've been in a continuous medical cycle since."

In his always kind and gentle manner, Russ reported, "Generally . . . the doctors don't want to talk about the root causes of the diseases. I've eaten a healthy diet for decades, worked outdoors on my farm, and kept in reasonably good shape.

"So what is it that triggered cancer in me, and not in the next person? And why is one of every three people now alive likely to be diagnosed with cancer? While this is a complex issue that makes it easier to focus on cures than prevention, our willingness to confront these root causes is going to be the difference between life and death or debilitating disease for our children and grandchildren. For their benefit, we'd better get busy."

I would add: We'd better pay attention to Russ Libby's work and legacy. Today's accolades must turn into tomorrow's actions.

Russ is of course best known for the seventeen years he spent building the Maine Organic Farmers and Gardeners Association into a national powerhouse, bringing new life to Maine's small farming community. He'd want me to give credit to all who helped, but each one of them knows who was driving the bus.

Many of us treasured the last year of Russ's life. He never gave up on life, never stopped working, never stayed home when he could be on the road, preaching the gospel of organic food and farming. He worked incredibly hard. I was amazed one day last spring to find Russ sitting in a legislative hearing room, preparing to testify. I quickly took a seat beside him, my favorite place to learn. Time spent with Russ was always a learning experience. He was incredibly smart and savvy.

Mary Anne, Russ's wife, is one of our town librarians, and one Saturday morning, I found Russ sitting in the children's room at the library while Mary Anne worked, apparently taking the opportunity to get out of the house. I sat there with him for a long time, learning.

While the stories and obituaries focused on his state and national work, it was right here in Mount Vernon that Russ excelled, at least for me. It was a privilege to work with him in the 1980s as we created the town's comprehensive plan. It focused, as you might imagine, on preserving farmland and open space.

Russ served our town in many key capacities, including as a selectman and a member of the school board. He negotiated contracts with our teachers in as fair and honest a manner as he conducted all of his other activities.

I am profoundly sorry that there will be no more learning experiences with Russ. One day he asked me how we liked the apples on the tree on our front lawn. I told him that red delicious were not particularly our favorite apples; he politely informed me that our tree was not a red delicious, but a historic variety that is now quite rare!

Linda and I missed Russ's memorial service last Saturday in Mount Vernon. We were in Brockton, Massachusetts, volunteering at My Brother's Keeper, selecting, wrapping, and delivering Christmas gifts to poor families. Russ would never have wanted us to cancel that trip on his behalf. And we won't forget him. Ever.

—Central Maine Newspapers (December 19, 2012)

Listening for Maine's Final Moo

When agriculture commissioner Walt Whitcomb started
dairy farming, Maine had 2,200 dairy farms. In 1991, I wrote
my first column in this space, lamenting the loss of Maine's
dairy farms. Six hundred farmers were still in the dairy business at that time.

In 2002, I wrote a sorrowful plea to save the 412 dairy farms
still clinging tenuously to their way of life, urging readers to
buy Maine milk, and to let the governor and legislature know
that dairy farms were important to them.

A few weeks ago, listening to legislators on the Agriculture,
Conservation, and Forestry Committee struggle with complex bills designed to help dairy farmers, I leaned forward and
asked former senator and dairyman John Nutting how many
dairy farmers we still have. His answer: 305. When the final
moo comes from the state's last cow, will anyone hear it?

Of course, nothing is this simple. Maine's remaining dairy
farmers are producing just as much milk as they did when
young Walt Whitcomb started milking cows. Each farm is
bigger, with a lot more cows. Maine has also led the nation
with its program that helps to stabilize the price that dairy
farmers get for their milk—but it wasn't enough to save our
small, rural dairy farms and farmers. And their loss has had a
devastating impact on communities, wildlife habitat, and open
space.

At one time, 75 percent of the 25,000 acres in my town of
Mount Vernon was cleared land. Today, we're down to 700
cleared acres—much of which is maintained by our last dairy

farmer, Dick Hall. Dick's mother Mildred once told me, "You have to be stupid to be a farmer," and Dick added, "Or crazy." I thought their comments were amusing at the time. Now they are coming true.

And the loss of dairy farms signals more than just the loss of our rural landscape. It's also the end of that marvelous rural attitude of independence and neighborliness, the place where doors are left unlocked, where a cash box sits by the roadside, inviting the purchase of corn and other vegetables.

It's the loss of a visual landscape of farm fields, stone walls, cows grazing on a hillside, a red-roofed barn dwarfing a white farmhouse. Also lost is a lot of critical wildlife habitat—for critters who depend on the edges of forests and fields.

I've never wanted to work as hard as farmers, but I sure am glad they are my neighbors. I'll always remember the morning Linda and I rushed from the house at four A.M. on the way to the hospital for Joshua's birth—and flew by Ray Hall on the North Road in his truck, heavily loaded with hay, on his way to some southern Maine farm.

Members of the legislature's Agriculture, Conservation, and Forestry Committee certainly understand all of this, but most committee members struggled in their recent work session to understand changes proposed for the dairy stabilization fund. Perhaps it's improved, but in one column I reported that 500 people administer the federal milk pricing program.

And as one committee member posed a series of questions about milk pricing, I remembered this long-ago statement from a Dairy Queen executive: "Milk is sort of like the international gold system. Only a handful of people claim to understand it, and most of them are lying."

In addition to the stabilization fund, the committee also wrestled with the details of a new Dairy Improvement Fund. Bless their hearts for trying. Two things jumped out at me: Seven committee members had bottles of soda in front of them. Soda! The enemy of milk! And the Dairy Improvement Fund would get its money from slot machine income. Lots of Mainers will lose money playing the slots, so we can try to save Maine's last dairy farms. Sad.

When our kids were small, we never missed the annual spring "cows coming out" experience at the Halls' dairy farm. Word would spread throughout the community, and so many people turned out that they eventually had to install bleachers. We'd all be there, beside the barn, when Dick slid open the green door in the early-morning dew and the cows emerged for the first time after a winter cooped up in the barn.

The cows danced, kicked, ran, mooed, and butted heads. It was an unforgettable sight, our spring ritual, the thing that passes for entertainment in our small rural town. That ritual is worth saving—even if it takes slot machines, I guess. Got milk?

—Central Maine Newspapers (April 18, 2012)

State Dessert an' Other Treats

Enjoying my newly designated state dessert for breakfast this morning, a juicy slice of blueberry pie, and looking forward to my afternoon now-official state treat, a good-size whoopie pie from the Isamax kitchen of Amy Bouchard in Farmingdale, I'm thinking about other state designations.

I did take note that although the legislature made these two designations, Governor Paul LePage refused to sign the bill, letting it become law without his signature. I better not see him with a whoopie pie in his hand.

Maine now has twenty-two designated symbols, and the sugar in this morning's pie is stimulating a lot more ideas for things that could be designated in the future. I got professional help with some of these from the designated Maine comedian, Gary Crocker. Here are a few suggestions.

We've got a lot of potential designations in food groups, starting with state mustard: Raye's Spicy Horseradish (made by the former Maine Senate president in his Eastport facility that uses the last mustard grindstone in the country).

- State suppah: Church.
- State meal: Beans, franks, coleslaw, and biscuits (with apologies to the makers of brown bread, which I don't like).
- State beer: Shipyard Export Ale.
- State export: Our children.
- State secret: Anything Paul LePage doesn't want you to know.

- State work of art: Labor mural that the governor removed from the Department of Labor—an easy choice!
- State retail store: Renys (with apologies to the deceased Mickey Marden).
- State sport: Complaining (about the weather, tourists, taxes, etc.).
- The state soft drink is Moxie, even though it's made in South Carolina. No one else drinks it but us. This opens up a bunch of ideas, such as:
- State sports team: Red Sox.
- State shopping mall: North Conway.
- State liquor store: Portsmouth.
- State recreational vehicle: ATV.
- State farm animal: Wild turkey (with special thanks to the dairy farmers who feed these birds—albeit unwillingly).
- The state cat is the coon cat, making it hard to believe we don't have a state dog. My nominee: Black lab.
- Dave Bell of the Maine Wild Blueberry Association tried to convince me that we could have a dozen designations for wild blueberries, from wine to muffins. I didn't have the heart to tell him any designation for muffin will be cranberry. Lin and I pick wild cranberries, and the muffins she makes with them are mouthwateringly fantastic—definitely my favorite.
- We have one state fish, the landlocked salmon, and two state heritage fish, the eastern brook trout and blueback char. But everyone knows the favorite fish of Maine anglers is the smallmouth bass (yes, yes, I know, another nonnative species—get over it).

- We have a state animal, the moose. But can you believe our other primary tourist attraction, the lobster, is not the state shellfish? Here's my suggestion: We'll line up the clammers and lobstermen and let them duke it out for the shellfish designation.
- State author: Stephen King (even if he has moved to Florida). I sat next to Steve in freshman creative writing class at the University of Maine. We both became writers, but he's done a little better with it.
- State game: Instant lottery.
- State slogan: Maine is open for business.
- Other state slogan: Kiss our butts.
- State tourist: Henry David Thoreau for environmentalists; Teddy Roosevelt for sportsmen. We might have awarded another tourist designation to Franklin Delano Roosevelt, but he passed right by our state to get to his summer place on Campobello Island, New Brunswick.
- We have a state insect, the honeybee. They really messed up this one. It obviously should be the blackfly. Believe it or not, we have a state floral emblem: pinecone and tassel. But the state flower should be the dandelion (yes, I know it's an invasive nonnative species, but it's pretty, pervasive, and we can eat it).
- We have a state song (no, it's not "The Maine Stein Song," but it should be), "State of Maine"; a state soil, Chesuncook; a state mineral, tourmaline; and even a state fossil, *Pertica quadrifaria*.
- Although we have a state bird, the chickadee, we ought to consider, given the state of our financial situation, changing it to the turkey vulture.

- Best state product we used to make is toothpicks, but it could be Bass shoes, Bates blankets, etc.
- Best Maine invention: The machine gun, invented by the Maxim boys of Dover-Foxcroft.
- And finally, the state nuisance: Red squirrel. But this one is wide open. I'm launching a line of T-shirts labeled MAINE STATE NUISANCE. The generic shirt comes with the photo of a red squirrel, but we'll be able to add the face of anyone you want. Could be your spouse. Could be your governor.

—Central Maine Newspapers (May 4, 2011)

A Life of Slow-Paced Riches

The pace of life accelerates. That was the inescapable conclusion reached after reading the front page of Saturday's newspaper. Just below a wonderful retrospective of the blizzard of 1952 was a story reporting that state police and game wardens are launching a crackdown on snowmobile recklessness.

When the 1952 blizzard dumped snow up to the roofs of some homes, toboggans and snowshoes were used to transport expectant mothers to the hospital. Today they'd be speeding along on a snowmobile. The massive and unexpected blizzard caused five deaths. Already this winter nine people have died on snowmobiles.

The memories shared by readers of that incredible snowstorm were enchanting: in Mount Vernon, twenty-five men shoveled three miles of road after the snowplow broke down so Mrs. Arthur Smith could get to the hospital to deliver her child; Knut Thorso pulled his wife Janice through the streets of Augusta on a toboggan to the hospital for the birth of their son Christian; Blanche Smith exited her house through a third-story window—that's how high the snow was—to have her baby on the toboggan in Rowena Hopkins' dooryard in Mount Vernon. Has a baby ever been born on a snowmobile?

Just four years old in 1952, I can reminisce only by looking at Dad's photos of Winthrop's Main Street, where the snowbanks reached nearly to the roof of Wilson's Dollar Stores where Dad worked.

My snowmobile memories are more vivid. Last week I almost killed a snowmobiler who dashed across the road in front of my Jeep near Flying Pond Variety Store in Mount Vernon. He never even glanced my way as I skidded to a stop about ten feet from his large sled.

"Snowmobiles are not toys," District Attorney Norman Croteau reported. "They can be dangerous." Warden Colonel Tim Peabody recognized that "snowmobiles are made to have fun on," but, "you can go out this afternoon, buy a sled, and go a hundred miles per hour without any training."

It's the pace of life that's killing us. Perhaps it's time to reevaluate our fun and games.

"Measures of Growth 2002," the eighth report of the Maine Economic Growth Council, reports that the "level of prosperity enjoyed by Maine people is relatively low and needs improvement." Among the measurements used to reach that conclusion is personal income. Personal income did not improve last year, leaving Maine in thirty-sixth place in the nation.

Maybe if they measured the number of snowmobiles per household, we'd get a better report. You know the story: Pass by any mobile home and you'll see two snowmobiles, an ATV, a satellite dish, and a couple of junker cars in the driveway.

These are the folks who are judged, in the Economic Growth Council's report, to be suffering a low level of prosperity. These folks are among the 33 percent judged to be making less than a livable wage.

They are also a caricature. There is real poverty in Maine, but there is also a level of prosperity that is never measured in these economic reports. I make a modest income but feel rich. Let me tell you why.

In my pocket is a smooth round pebble from the beach at West Quoddy Head Light. The pebble reminds me of my mom and my Lubec coastal heritage. Holding the rock in my hand, I can see that rugged coastline where my great-grand-father kept the Light for thirty years, and where my sense of ownership makes me a rich man. You and I own that piece of Maine, the easternmost point in the United States.

Meandering outside my window is Hopkins Stream. Black ducks float on the still water this morning. "My" bald eagle has not yet passed by, but he will be along soon. In the summer, I slip a kayak into the moving water and float five miles without seeing a soul. Lunker bass grab my Banjo Minnow while deer frolic in the streamside meadows. I feel like a very rich man.

Today, pretending I'm in the 1952 blizzard, I'll slip on a pair of snowshoes (the old wooden ones—no new aluminum shoes for me) and stomp downstream. I am likely to see fisher tracks, and perhaps glimpse a great horned owl. Dozens of ducks will be noted, and I will move quietly along just outside the deer-wintering area, taking note of the different sizes of tracks. "My" deer are doing well this winter. I am a wealthy man.

A photo of Dad and me fishing at our beloved Sourdnahunk Lake is on the wall above my desk. Already, I look forward to our first trip in May to catch the eager trout right after ice-out. We are rich men. Often, as I stand in some spectacular place in Maine, hunting, fishing, or bird-watching, I ask myself, "I wonder what the rich people are doing today?" And I laugh.

Even as our lives accelerate, our prosperity comes at a slower pace. We may never measure up to the level of prosperity enjoyed elsewhere, but no one should doubt the richness of a Maine life.

—*Kennebec Journal* (February 20, 2002)

Disasters Make Good Neighbors

In the eighty-eighth hour without power, on a very cold winter night, Lin called me to the bank of windows in my home office on the east side of the house. A full moon hovered over the treetops on the opposite shore of Hopkins Pond, splashing light across the pond and up into our young oak tree, still proudly hanging on to all of its ice-laden branches.

The moonlight sparkled brightly off each ice cake on the tree. We stood quietly, awestruck. The scene was breathtaking—as was the temperature in the unheated office. We retreated to our sanctuary beside the kitchen cookstove.

It's been nearly a century since our two-hundred-year-old Cape was called upon to house its residents in this manner. The Ice Storm of 1998 took us back in time. And just as it was back then, neighbors helped each other with hot food, kind hearts, fuel, and good old conversation.

Amazingly and thankfully, communication was easy. Community Telephone's lines never went down, radio stations switched to all-talk formats to pass on tips and news, and—well beyond our expectations—the *Kennebec Journal* showed up in our roadside box every morning. Good job, people.

Of course, I was unprepared for the devastation and the long power outage. But a shed full of seasoned wood kept the fireplaces going and us warm. The cookstove allowed Lin to prepare fabulous meals. As the refrigerator and freezer gave out, we ate more and more to keep up with thawing food. It was gluttony. Lin's apple-raspberry-cranberry pies were

mouthwatering masterpieces. And she didn't complain when I
ate it for breakfast.

I failed to have the Aladdin lamps ready, and the old lamp
mantel gave out the first dark night. But the next day, as I
was standing in the road, videotaping trees snapping in half,
neighbors Ron and Nancy LaRue drove by on their way to
Farmington for horse feed.

"Need anything?" asked Ron.

"Yes, we do," said I, mentioning the lamp mantel. An hour
later the best neighbors anyone could hope for drove in with
the mantel, which gave us one night of fabulous light until I
tried to repair the wick, busting the lamp and grossly disappointing my family.

Eggs were in short supply at our house on Day 2, so Lin
called Ralph Hopkins to ask if he had eggs to sell. He did. She
told Ralph we'd walk the mile to his farm later in the morning to pick them up. We didn't dare drive. Conditions were
treacherous between our house and Ralph's. Ten minutes later
Ralph drove in with two dozen eggs, and he refused to accept
anything more than his usual 85 cents per dozen. Another
great neighbor.

It was a candlelight adventure until the bitter-cold weather
set in. Afraid our pipes had burst on Sunday night, I called
Augusta Fuel and my friend John Tyler Monday morning.

"Help!" I said.

They'd heard it before. As the receptionist courteously
explained, it would be forty hours before they could come and
help us. I requested a phone call from John for advice. Five
minutes later he called and told me how to drain my pipes.
Josh and I spent a couple hours doing that.

When John and his helper showed up Tuesday night, we were mighty glad to see them. And his compressor gave us good news—no frozen pipes. Although he hadn't eaten all day, John rushed past the offered steaming hot beef stroganoff to get to more desperate customers in Fayette. Incredible dedication.

Anyone who said a storm like this offered a nice opportunity to sit by the fire and read was nuts. It was chores, chores, and more chores, chopping and hauling wood from the shed, collecting flushing water in buckets from the stream, getting drinking water from the Fire Department—a beehive of support and information, command central in Mount Vernon.

Bob and Leslie Grenier kept their stores open with generators, although they lost everything in their freezers that they couldn't give away, and managed as the week progressed to round up key supplies like batteries, extension cords, and lamps. They even had candles, which we could find nowhere else.

At church on Sunday, Larry and Nancy Perkins, whose power had been restored in Readfield, volunteered to take everything in our big freezer, which was about to give out. They had lost their own freezer full of food, and cleaned it out to take in ours. Generous acts like this were common.

And how about those flatlanders! From West Virginia, Maryland, Pennsylvania, New Jersey, Rhode Island, and more, they came singly and in caravans to provide life-saving services. Many were in Maine for the first time, but saw nothing more than twenty-hour workdays amid arctic conditions. Governor Angus King should invite them and their families back in July for a lobster bake and a proper thank-you.

As I write this column on my portable computer at the home of my in-laws, Ivy and Lew Hillier in Winthrop, whose power was restored yesterday, Lin, Josh, Hilary, and I are in our 174th hour without power. We continue to be patient and salute the heroes and Good Samaritans, the linemen and electricians, plumbers and plowers and postmen and public works crews, food banks and firemen, tree trimmers and rescue squads, great neighbors and good friends. From adversity, we drew strength from each other. Thank you, all.

—*Kennebec Journal* (January 19, 1998)

This Old House

The Statler Brothers must have known about my house when they sang "This Old House." One verse goes like this: "This old house is getting shaky, this old house is getting old, this old house lets in the rain, this old house lets in the cold."

Our center-chimney Cape was built in 1790, so it's not just getting old; it *is* old. In the torrential rain a couple weekends ago, water flowed right down the side of our chimney and spread along a bedroom ceiling.

One end of the house sits on stones with just a three-foot crawl space between us and the ground. The wind whips up through the wide pine boards on the floor, and the pipes in the crawl space freeze anytime the temps go below zero. Last winter standing water in the bathtub actually froze solid.

Another verse of the Statler Brothers' song also describes our house well: "This old house is afraid of thunder, this old house is afraid of storms, this old house just groans and trembles when the night wind flings its arms."

Our old house has good reason to fear thunderstorms. An old fellow from Auburn used to visit us each summer. He was born in this house in 1900 in the "borning room" that is now part of our living room, and lived here for eleven years. He remembered his father talking on a phone in what is now our dining room and being blown across the room by a strike of lightning.

I kind of know how he felt. Last June lightning struck again, blowing out most of our appliances, toasting our TVs, and knocking out electric circuits. The garage-door opener—an

ancient Sears model that had worked flawlessly for decades—
took a hit and gave up the ghost. The new model has been a
nightmare. It is apparently incompatible with our old garage
door—a sturdy model that has survived all three of my
attempts to drive the Jeep out without raising it.

This new opener has these ridiculous safety devices at the
bottom of the door to make sure the door doesn't close on top
of me. Well, now the door goes down and the door goes up,
entirely irrespective of my wishes. So I've got a good excuse
now for driving through the door—except it's never really
down. It seems to prefer the up and open position.

But it's the last half of that particular verse of the Statler
Brothers' song that really hits home, so to speak: "This old
house is getting feeble, this old house is needin' paint, just like
me it's tuckered out." Amen.

The song's chorus captures my immediate situation: "Ain't
gonna need this house no longer, ain't gonna need this house
no more; ain't got time to fix the shingles, ain't got time to fix
the floor; ain't got time to oil the hinges, nor to mend the win-
dowpane; ain't gonna need this house no longer, I'm getting
ready to meet the saints."

Having celebrated my fifty-seventh birthday on Saturday,
I'm hoping the saints are willing to wait a while for this tuckered soul to join them. But I'm not sure the house can do that.
Fall chores are almost overwhelming, and I ain't got time.
The energy-saving tips printed recently in the newspaper are
appreciated—but who the heck is going to put plastic on the
inside of their windows?

Okay, I'll confess. I've got a plastic storm window on the
backside of the house where the neighbors won't be scandalized

by my cheapness. We put our best storms on the front—and they're really nice-looking if you don't look too close. These are old wooden storm windows, and most have very little putty left holding the windowpanes in place.

One species isn't waiting to secure their place in our house. Armies of mice are moving in with us now. Up in the attic, they skitter across the living-room ceiling while we watch TV. A feeding frenzy goes on at night in the cold storage cellar, and sometimes right upstairs in our kitchen. One fall I caught twenty-eight mice in one kitchen drawer.

Skunks and coons check out the crawl space as a potential hibernating home. They remind me of the fall I found a sala-mander in the basement. You just never know who you're sharing an old house with.

There's just one part of the Statler Brothers' song that doesn't ring true with me, and that's when they sing, "My huntin' days are over, I ain't gonna hunt the coon no more; Gabriel done brought in the chariot, when the wind blew down the door."

The doors to our house still stand, and I'll be out hunting on the opening day of deer season, even though the fall chores remain undone. This old house will just have to wait.

—Central Maine Newspapers (October 19, 2005)

Update: We fully insulated the old house a few years ago, and cut our oil consumption by a thousand gallons. We've also made many other improvements, including new windows and doors. The old place is looking pretty good these days.

The Hermit's Life

He lived off the grid as well as off his neighbors. He robbed Peter to pay himself. And now he's more famous than any of Maine's political leaders. The story of the Hermit of Rome, Maine, went worldwide.

Maine law enforcement officers missed a good opportunity when they cleaned out Christopher Knight's encampment. People would have come to Maine and paid good money to see it. Some would have paid to stay there.

I told Sharon Wood, who does a great job with the art and layout of these newspapers, that this would have been a great Travelin' Maine(rs) column for Linda and me. We could have stayed at the encampment, stolen from the neighbors, and written about the experience. Sharon suggested we could call this the Travelin' Steal(ers). Before you know it, people would have been paying $100 a night to stay there. After all, the food is free.

It is astonishing that the Hermit could have avoided detection for twenty-seven years and more than a thousand burglaries. I was amused when the first reference to him reported that he lived in the "wilderness of Rome." There is no wilderness in Rome, or even next door in Mount Vernon, where I live. Later references downgraded the wilderness to woods.

My hunting buddies and I could have found this guy in a morning of deer hunting. The woods around here are scoured every November as we search for deer. I've noted the map Sharon added to some of the news stories about the hermit, and pinpointed his spot. If no deer hunter got there in

76

the last twenty-seven years, that's where I want to hunt this November!

So far, it appears that his thefts were focused on nonresidents. Might he have been reading too many Bert and I stories that make fun of our friends from away? Or is it simply a reflection of the fact that nonresidents own most of the lakefront property hereabouts?

Of course, everyone wants to know his motives for such an isolated and careless (some would say "carefree," but I doubt it) lifestyle. The Hermit could have lived a more comfortable life living off the rest of us legally—using local and state aid, shopping at the food pantries, partaking from programs offered by the nonprofit community.

His choice of lifestyle is really all about us. He didn't like us. He wanted to avoid us. Some days, reading these words, you might feel the same. He preferred his books and his all-the-time quiet time. As an inveterate reader and someone with a very busy life, I get that. Now, he gets to mingle with the worst of us, in jail. That is probably not improving his opinion of us.

Who among us hasn't fantasized about chucking it all and heading into the woods? This is what will make the Hermit's book so appealing. It'll be a fantasy, of course, because the reality was a hard and lonely life, full of cold, discomfort, thievery, and guilt (we hope). It's intriguing simply because he got away with it for so long.

I was going to call it a deprived life, but I'll bet he doesn't see it that way. And that's the saddest part of his story.

Coincidentally, I have been participating in a Wednesday-night book group at church, focused on *Bread in the Wilderness* by Pastor Kenneth Carter Jr. The back cover reports, "Christians know that we often live in the wilderness—a place of difficulty and even danger—and yet we also believe that there is bread in the wilderness."

This took on a whole new meaning when I read the account of the Hermit of Rome. Bread in the wilderness, indeed.

As we ended our book discussion on the final night, the epilogue recounted the story of Moses, whose father-in-law notices that Moses is overwhelmed and tells him, "What you are doing is not good. You will surely wear yourself out . . . The task is too heavy . . . You cannot do it alone" (Exodus 18:17–18).

If you are reading this column, Christopher, I commend this chapter of the Bible to you.

—Central Maine Newspapers (April 17, 2013)

Part II:
Hunting, Fishing,
and Other Outdoor Fun

Hunting Is My Heritage

The canoe paddle dips silently into the calm waters of Hopkins Stream, mist hiding the shoreline ahead, allowing us to sneak up to three buffleheads that take off in surprise. A muskrat slowly meanders toward shore, in no hurry to get away. He steps up on land and gazes out at us.

We quietly exit the canoe, quickly glancing at the oak knoll in front of us where deer have been feeding heavily. Fresh deer sign is everywhere as we trudge three hundred yards to our ground blind on the top of a small ridge, overlooking the oaks.

This morning Dad and I choose to sit together. He looks one way, I look the other. It's quiet, comforting, cleansing for the mind and body. I've been known to nap in the woods during deer season. We enjoy coffee and muffins, content to sit in anticipation.

Anticipation that a deer may appear at any moment is the very best part of the hunt, and we do a lot of anticipating. This particular morning, that's all we do. No deer appear, although later in the morning I jump one in a thick fir stand, hearing the crack and commotion of an escaping whitetail without casting my eyes on the critter.

I pause to enjoy the smell of the firs, the cushion of the mossy forest floor, the skittering of red squirrels, and the sharp taste of my fresh Maine apple. A chickadee alights two feet from my face, unafraid. I remember the time an ermine ran up my leg and arm while I sat on the ground, leaning against a tree. Last year I was mesmerized by two fishers cavorting along through my woodlot. They never saw me. You see amazing things while hunting. As I move into an open area with a parcel of standing dead trees, a magnificent pileated woodpecker cries out, then lands thirty yards away. Wow! What a bird!

This morning, I am thinking about a letter in yesterday's *Kennebec Journal*, criticizing the paper for printing photographs of young hunters with their deer.

"Children should not be taught that it is their privilege to hunt and kill. If killing a defenseless animal for 'sport' is your bonding time with a child, you may want to take a look at the negative impact this may have on your child. In time, it will destroy the child's ability to show empathy for wildlife," wrote this gentleman.

I'm sure glad Dad didn't think this way when I was growing up. He raised me to be a Maine sportsman, and my times spent hunting and fishing with Dad are my most memorable childhood experiences. Fortunately, we're still doing that today.

I am living proof that hunting does not destroy the "ability to show empathy for wildlife." I love the critters in the forest, all of them, and spend thousands of hours every year watching them. A few I shoot and eat, respectful of them and what they contribute to my life and my table. I am not a killer; I am a hunter. And I do understand the difference.

There is no way to convey this to those who believe hunting is, as this letter writer reported, "shameful." Yet we have so much in common. "For me," he writes, "the sighting of a deer is a marvel of God's existence." It is for me, too!

I meander into a stand of tall hemlocks, taking a seat on an old stump, pondering what specifically God would expect of me these days. What does He expect me to eat? How does He expect me to get that food? Alas, I am not nearly wise enough to have the answers. It must be nice to have all the answers. I seek them, oftentimes in the solitude of the woods, but few are provided to me.

Later that night, about ten P.M., a doe and lamb eat grass on our front lawn, and I get within ten feet of them, only the wall and window separating us. I watch them for twenty minutes, captivated. I have no interest in shooting them. They seem to know that, and stare back at me, unafraid.

Perhaps this is the answer: I know when to shoot, and when not to shoot. I do not kill indiscriminately, but only with purpose, with legal right, with respect for the animal. Perhaps this is what God would expect.

I can only hope so. Because I can no more stop hunting than I can stop breathing.

—Central Maine Newspapers (November 22, 2006)

Heart-Stopping Hunting

Each November I clear out my head in the woods, in pursuit of a white-tailed deer. The serenity and solitude of the Maine forest eliminates a year's worth of worry and stress. Or so I thought.

Last week an Associated Press story, headlined HUNTERS' HEARTS AT RISK, warned that the excitement of the chase is dangerous to my health.

"During a typical deer season in Michigan, about a dozen hunters die of heart attacks," reported AP writer Daniel Q. Haney. Hospital researchers found that even the sight of a deer sends the heartbeat soaring, sometimes doubling. One guy's heartbeat shot up from 78 to 168 beats per minute when he spotted a ten-point buck. I believe it. We call it *buck fever*. It also causes the arms and legs to quiver.

"We have shown that hunting is an extremely strenuous activity and might be dangerous for some people," concluded a researcher.

I have more bad news for them: My heartbeat races when I hear a squirrel rustling in the frozen leaves. Sounds just like a deer coming my way. When a tree snaps fifty yards away in the bog, I get excited. Walking along a deer trail, my glasses fog up. At 10 degrees in a howling wind, I work up a sweat. I'm in big trouble health-wise, apparently. And all this time I thought I was relaxing!

What the study didn't measure was the effect of losing ten pounds during the deer season from all that walking, of the toning up of muscles not used the previous eleven months, of the tremendous improvement in mental health which occurs after a week in the woods.

Opening day, on November 2, found Dad and I hunkered down in the oaks where a bountiful crop of acorns was drawing feeding deer. As I hid behind the roots of a blown-down hemlock, overlooking a large ground scrape left by a sizable, make-the-heart-race buck to mark his territory and attract a doe, I saw something brown bounding through the woods behind me.

With my heart apparently racing, I waited for the animal to step into the open. When it did, I marveled at a very large male fisher. When it got within twenty feet, I moved slightly to alert it to my presence. Fishers can be vicious, and I didn't want it walking right into my blind.

The fisher spotted my movement immediately and jumped right into the air, twisted around, and was out of the clearing in a single bound. I wonder if they've ever tested the heartbeats of animals when they spy a hunter? Do they ever drop dead? What a way to bag a big buck!

"Yup, I was just standing there. That big buck stepped out in front of me. I said 'Hello, Mr. Buck,' and he dropped dead right in his tracks."

Later in the morning, Dad sat in a new chair we'd installed on top of a large boulder overlooking our bog, and I plowed around inside the bog, looking for the Big Swamp Buck (there's always a Big Swamp Buck in these stories—to get the reader's heart pounding). Careful now; keep calm. I don't want to lose any readers here.

A whole herd of deer jumped up in front of me, and it's a wonder I didn't drop dead right there in the bog. They all pranced out to Dad—three does—and stood around in front of his seat. Lucky I didn't lose him that morning, I guess. But he remained calm. Neither of us won doe permits this year.

By then it was nine-thirty and time for coffee and blueberry muffins. We reminisced about past seasons and shared a great morning. Then Dad headed down to the stream while I hiked south to take a stand on a ridge which runs parallel to the stream. I had just taken my position behind a huge pine when a shot rang out down along the stream.

Ten minutes later I gazed left and spotted a nice buck trotting through the woods about fifty yards to my left. The gleam of his white rack told me I could shoot, so the rifle came up, the safety came off, and when he stopped, I hit him. I can verify the study by telling you my heart was pounding at this point. The buck took off and I took two more shots before he dropped.

Hauling him off that ridge almost gave me a heart attack, so I know the study is accurate. We hauled him down to the stream and brought him home in the canoe. That lean venison will repair the damage this experience did to my poor old heart.

If I'm ever found dead of a heart attack in the woods, please assume that I went out smiling at a huge buck, the last thing I saw in this world. What a way to go.

—*Kennebec Journal* (2004)

Hunting Fatality

The grief is unimaginable. An eighteen-year-old girl is dead, a muzzle-loading hunter responsible. On Thursday, December 8, 2006, behind her home in Paris, Maine, Megan Ripley was killed.

Anger is to be expected, no matter what the circumstances, and hunting is sure to suffer the backlash of community concerns. On Friday, December 9, I was besieged by media calls, wanting my comments on the shooting—not unexpected given my role as executive director of the Sportsman's Alliance of Maine. I returned no calls, certain that anything I said would sound defensive and be entirely unsatisfactory.

With a deep sense of irony, I went hunting. Sitting in the woods, surrounded by snow-covered trees, I offered a prayer for the Ripley family and the hunter and his family. With plenty of time to think about this terrible tragedy, in that peaceful setting, I reached the following conclusion.

The hunter made an inexcusable mistake. Here's what Maine's target identification law requires: "While hunting, a hunter may not shoot at a target without, at that point in time, being certain that it is the wild animal and wild bird sought. A reasonable and prudent hunter always bears the risk of loss of legitimate prey to avoid the risk of the destruction of human life.

"A reasonable and prudent hunter neither disregards the risk of causing the death of another human being nor fails to be aware of that risk as a consequence of misidentification. A reasonable and prudent hunter . . . bases identification upon obtaining an essentially unobstructed view of the head and torso of the potential target. This visual sighting is the most critical target-determining factor . . . [and must exist when] the hunter takes aim and is making the final preparation to shoot."

The law requires other factors to be considered as well, including "the distance to the target, surrounding or intervening terrain and cover, lighting and weather conditions, the hunter's own ability to hear and see, the hunter's own experience, and the proximity of other persons in the hunter's immediate vicinity."

There is more to this law, which is really quite specific about what must be considered before the hunter shoots at a deer. But to me, the most important thing is the requirement that we pass up a shot at what we think might be a deer, perhaps are even certain is a deer, rather than risk harm to another person.

This requires us to pass up deer when the shot would go toward and might reach a house or road. It is absolutely essential that the hunter know where his bullet will go if the deer is missed.

Mark Latti, the very capable spokesman for Maine's Department of Inland Fisheries and Wildlife, had the unenviable job of commenting on this tragedy, and I thought his words were just right. He noted the exceptional safety record of hunting in Maine; this shooting death was only the second instance in eighteen years where a nonhunter was killed by a hunter, and the first hunting-related death since 2004.

In the 1940s and '50s, as many as twenty hunting fatalities occurred each season. Sportsmen are justifiably proud to have made hunting one of the safest outdoor activities in Maine.

But these words of Latti's rang especially true for me: "This is not to sugarcoat this tragedy by any means. Because that's what this is—a horrific tragedy, and I was just sickened by it—all of us here were." That's what I would have said, if I had returned those media calls.

Already, the reaction against hunting has been strong. Some say they'll post their land. Others call for a reduced deer season. Many noted that the public should be made more aware that a two-week muzzle-loading season follows the regular November firearms deer season. And some said the public should be required to wear blaze orange during the deer seasons, just like hunters are.

But here's the bottom line: While it is recommended that you wear blaze orange during the firearms seasons, you should not have to do that to be safe in your own woods, or anywhere else.

On December 6 at the Capitol, Senate President Beth Edmonds, surprised to learn I was still hunting deer in December, said she was unaware of the muzzle-loading season. I told her not to worry; she was very safe outdoors in Maine, regardless of the season.

I was right. And I was wrong.

—Central Maine Newspapers (December 13, 2006)

Of Pheasants and Fathers

The crisp autumn afternoon, the stiff point of the English setter, the explosion of a pheasant from the tall grass, the heft of the shotgun as I brought it to my shoulder, the crack which cut the cool air, and the folding of the colorful bird, followed quickly by the dog's retrieve, set my course for a lifetime. Dad's presence right behind me reinforced the hunting tradition and all its glory.

On my office wall, I still have the photo of us with the setter and my first pheasant. I look awfully small, but I must have been twelve years old or so. In high school, Dad started me trapping. No paper route for me.

I got up before dawn to check my trapline along the Waugan, an inlet to Annabessacook Lake in my hometown of Winthrop. Of course, Dad accompanied me, and the fog on my face, the breathtaking sunrises, the quiet dip of the paddle in the water, the winding course of the stream, and my exhilaration at finding a "rat" in a trap, are still vivid. I earned some valuable spending money and learned a lot.

Forty years later, I returned the favor and introduced Dad to turkey hunting. After a year of hunting turkeys myself, I knew he'd love the challenge, camaraderie, and interchanges with the tom turkeys.

This year, on opening day of the May season on turkeys, we sat at the edge of a Mount Vernon cornfield as I "talked turkey" to a tom down in the woods. Eventually, the tom moved out into the field and headed for our decoys. Dad shot him at about twenty yards, a hefty twenty-one-pound bird. I retrieved the bird. We haven't had setters in a long time. What we do have is a generational bond, forged in the fields and forests and on the lakes and rivers of Maine.

It's often like this. Thirty years after my first pheasant provided a tasty meal for my family, I heard Dad's rifle shots ring out on a spring-like November morning from his deer stand about three hundred yards above my own along a Mount Vernon tote road. A half-hour later, as he trudged down the road toward me, the look on his face told me the story. I knew before he spoke that he'd filled his tag. He wore the same look I saw in the pheasant field so many years ago.

Hunting and fishing have always been my links to Dad. Time spent together in the woods and on the waters is priceless—beyond the comprehension of those who are less privileged.

That I became perhaps the state's most recognized advocate for sportsmen, and an outdoor writer and television show host, is no coincidence. It was my destiny from that first step behind the English setter with Dad. He set my course for life on that very first morning afield.

It's been a good life, for both of us. And for that, on this Father's Day, I am so grateful.

My Kids

I wrote the Father's Day tribute above for my dad in 1990, for the *Kennebec Journal,* and later that year, combined some of the elements of that column with a bit about my own kids. Here's what I wrote about my kids.

My son Joshua is eight years old. He has already sat patiently in a duck blind (although he brought along a book to read—which I encouraged him to do). He loves nature and has a real reverence for it. I don't know yet if he'll be a hunter, although I surely hope so. Yesterday, when he stepped off the school bus and ran to my side to excitedly report he had just seen not one but two bucks in a nearby field, I caught a glimpse of that certain look. I think he's got what it takes.

My oldest daughter Rebekah is a student at Bowdoin College. No hope there. She tolerates my hunting, but will never be a part of it.

My youngest daughter Hilary is five years old. She informed her mother last year that she was going hunting with Dad, and he was going to get her a gun, because they made small guns just her size. I had not told her that. How on earth did she get that message from me? Perhaps, because we had never talked about it, Hilary just assumed that girls hunt. At least, she assumes that she can hunt too.

Will I take her? Well, the other night at the supper table, Hilary piped up and said she was never going to hunt. When she saw my face drop, she laughed and said, "Just kidding, Dad!"

We'll see.

—Most of this column appeared in *The Maine Times* (December 21, 1990)

Update: Josh shot a deer when he was sixteen years old—his one and only. He has a busy life, no time for hunting, but he is an avid angler. Hilary learned to fly-fish when she was eight years old, and continues to (occasionally) join me on the water. She never hunted. Rebekah and her husband Patrick have given us two wonderful grandsons, now ages six and nine. I am working on them! Dad is ninety years old. We've been hunting together for 53 years.

Fiftieth-Birthday River Rescue

Fiftieth birthday one day. Rescued from the Kennebec River the next.

It was that kind of week. Achieving the half-century mark, one would expect to contemplate life's meaning. Have I accomplished enough, been all that I can be, to justify five decades on this planet?

A family dinner celebration at an Augusta restaurant demonstrated what is important in life, and I built on that with a fishing expedition the next afternoon on the Kennebec River.

As rescues go, it wasn't all that daring—but the turnout and response from the Augusta Fire Department was impressive, if terribly embarrassing. Stripers were few and far between, so I motored the boat up to the Edwards Dam a couple of times, up- and downriver, looking for those telltale splashes that signal active stripers. The tide was very high and a lot of water was coming down the river, with a current so strong my anchor wouldn't hold.

Then the gas tank ran dry. Floating freely and fast downriver, I quickly switched to the other full tank, but the motor wouldn't start. Panicked, I gave it a lot of gas—too much, as it turned out. Speeding past the railroad bridge, nearly colliding with an abutment, and cursing the fact that I'd left my paddle at home, I pulled and pulled and pulled the starter cord. Nothing.

Finally, after sweeping under the old downtown bridge, the anchor took hold, pulling me to a stop right in the middle of the river, about even with the boat launch where this adventure had started. I caught my breath, tried the motor again unsuccessfully, and looked wistfully toward shore. There wasn't a single boat on the river, but surely someone would come along who could tow me to shore.

Grabbing a rod, I decided to make the most of my dilemma and started fishing. Periodically I'd try the motor again, with no luck. No luck fishing, either. After an hour, with no boats in sight, a young fellow on shore in the Water Street parking lot shouted out, "Do you need help?"

After thinking about it a minute, I decided I was ready to go home and could indeed use a tow. I knew the fire department had a boat, and thought perhaps they might be willing to help me out. "Yes, I need a tow to shore," I shouted back.

About two minutes later, sirens and alarms went off all over the city. *Oh God, please don't let that be for me,* I prayed.

Too late for prayer. The troops were coming. If all of Water Street was on fire, I doubt there'd be a bigger response. Up and down the hillsides of the city on both sides of the river, sirens wailed. A fire truck pulled in to the riverside boat launch, then an ambulance, then another ambulance, and more trucks than I could count.

One fireman ran to shore and began scanning the river. Sheepishly, I tried to ignore him. Then it occurred to me that they must think someone was in real trouble on the river.

Using hand signals, I conveyed my need of a tow to shore. With a short wave, acknowledging his understanding, the fireman pulled out his walkie-talkie and called in the boat crew. But no one left. Indeed, a crowd had gathered by now, pulled in by the sirens and excitement of a river rescue.

Gosh, was I embarrassed. As the rescue boat pulled alongside, one wide-grinning fireman inquired, "How's the fishing?"

"Not good," I replied. For a brief moment, I fantasized that no one would recognize me. But as I stepped onto the dock, fireman Dan Guimond, who I know well, greeted me with a, "Hi, George!"

"Dan," I said, "today I'm Harry Vanderweide, if you don't mind."

"Well, Harry's boat does look like yours," he kindly replied.

Later, with the boat on Maranacook Lake's calmer waters, I got the gas working through and the motor purring. But I haven't shown my face on the river since the rescue. I have spent some time contemplating the future and looking into the past, considering how fortunate we are to have firemen and rescue squads, ready to respond promptly when needed.

There's a lot of rescuing that needs to be done these days. I'm starting to feel disoriented in a world that's changing so fast. Last Tuesday's *Kennebec Journal* reported that this November, only 150,000 resident hunters will join me for Maine's fabled deer hunt. That's 75,000 fewer than hunted Maine's woods in 1981. It's also the smallest percentage of the state's population with big-game hunting licenses, just 15.8 percent, since I was born.

Some days I feel like I'm at anchor in the middle of a swift river, life moving quickly past, unable to get my motor going. But please, no more rescues.

—*Kennebec Journal* (October 28, 1998)

Loving Alaska with Linda

I fell in love with Kamishak, and my wife was there to see it. Kami wasn't my only new love that week—just the first. Little Ku stole my heart one day, the more full-bodied Moraine another. But I kept coming back to Kami, and made her my final choice.

On a weeklong vacation at Rainbow River Lodge in Iliamna, Alaska, our first look at Kami was from high above her in a floatplane. She's a big coastal river, but not distinguishable from other Alaskan beauties from the air. However, once we started upriver in a boat and spotted a huge brown bear on the first gravel bar, the Kami's special allure grabbed me.

By the time our guide beached the boat at our first fishing location, we'd seen—up close—ten brown bears, including a sow with two cubs, and I'd used up my first roll of film. If you're fishing the Kami, bring your camera.

In three days there, we saw seventeen, twenty, and twenty-five bears, respectively—and we did respect them. They fished beside us like longtime angling buddies, wrestled each other, frolicked in the river, and generally ignored us. It was hard to ignore them.

Even harder to ignore were the fish: huge coho salmon, called silvers, stacked like logs in calm pools, resting on their way up the rapid river to spawning grounds; colorful Dolly Varden trout resting in every riffle of fast water, feeding on salmon eggs.

I was particularly delighted to find we could catch silvers on the surface, using a large fly that we dragged across the top of the water—sort of like fishing for bass. This worked each morning for a short while, and then we'd switch to subsurface flies—still using floating line on our 8-weight rods.

And guess what: The fly of choice was a Green Clouser—the same fly I employ for trout in Maine! You'd drift the Clouser just under the surface, draw it past the silver of choice—because almost all of this is sight-fishing—and hold your breath when the fish turned to gulp the fly. Often these fish would follow the fly for a distance, sometimes waiting to take it almost at your feet. Wow!

Linda and I battled hefty eleven- and twelve-pound silvers all morning that first day with Kami, then switched to Dollies to rest our aching shoulders, getting—no exaggeration—a fish on every other cast, with many over twenty inches long. My biggest Dolly was a six-pound brute.

For Dollies we used 5-weight rods and a bead that resembled a pink or red salmon egg. It was important to get the color of the bead right—just one of many reasons that the employment of a guide makes a lot of sense.

Eager to take our flies, and tough fighters, the green-tinted Dollies are too often ignored in these world-renowned salmon and rainbow trout waters. But we loved their eagerness and their fight, and we took every opportunity to fish for them.

Of course, we'd traveled all the way from Maine to this first-class Alaskan wilderness lodge to catch giant rainbow trout, so our love affair with the Kamishak and her bears and silvers and Dollies was an unexpected surprise.

The rainbows did not disappoint. Many exceeded twenty inches in length, and either of the two twenty-seven-inch, eight-pound fish I caught—one on the intriguing Little Ku

(Nanuktuk River), the other from the bigger Moraine Creek—would have been the thrill of a lifetime for any avid angler.

For three days on the rainbow rivers, we used light, 5-weight fly rods, stood surrounded by spawning red and pink salmon amidst stunning scenery in cold rushing rivers, peered into the water to see gigantic rainbows lying in wait, drifted our flies past the selected fish, watched as the fish grabbed our fly, set the hook, and took a deep breath—so we could yell *Fish on!*

A relative novice with a fly rod, experienced only with small Maine brook trout, with one trip to Quebec where she caught some big landlocked salmon, Linda was somewhat stressed, worried that she would not cast well enough or be able to land these big Alaskan brutes.

But with good advice from our guides, she had no problem at all, learned a great deal, experienced more catching of big fish in a week than you'd get in a lifetime of fly fishing in Maine, and landed as many of her fish as even the most experienced anglers that week (including yours truly, who had a hard time learning that you can't just horse these fish in).

Traveling to other states and countries is always interesting. Traveling to Alaska is so much more—exciting, inspiring, with jaw-dropping beauty, massive mountain chains harboring glistening glaciers, high-country tundra, a stunning coastline, rivers, lakes, and ponds of all sizes—all on a scale that is unimaginable to anyone in the Lower Forty-Eight.

And did I mention the bears? I am amazed by the photos of Lin calmly casting her fly while a huge bear—sporting a light brown coat—stood nearby, watching her. She went from a state of terror about the bears to complete nonchalance. Well, honestly, she was wary but not worried.

Rainbow River Lodge managers Chad and Nicole Hewitt might have missed the first Alaskan gold rush, but today, there's still plenty of gold in the fishery found in this state's coastal and inland waters, thanks to savvy fisheries management, good research, and an understanding of what spectacular fishing can do for a state's economy and people. No rainbow trout in this entire area can be killed. It's all catch-and-release angling for trout with barbless hooks. Three salmon per day may be kept, and the lodge staff fillets, freezes, and packs them for you.

Lin and I also rode the train from Anchorage to Denali National Park, where Mount McKinley peeked at us through the smoke generated from fires that have burned more than five million acres in Alaska this year. In this stunning national park, we saw lots of caribou, mountain sheep, grizzlies, and three of the biggest bull moose you could ever hope to see (Alaskan moose are about a third larger than Maine's).

But it's Rainbow River Lodge and the fishing that I will never forget. This was the best fishing I have ever enjoyed in my life. The lodge offers my kind of wilderness experience: gorgeous comfortable cabins, hot showers, gourmet food, superb service, super-friendly staff, gracious hosts—all in a family environment where baby Hewitt joined us every evening for dinner.

This is a fly-out lodge, where—every day—you are able to fly to your selected river to fish for your favorite species. Admittedly, this is pampered angling—until the first big rainbow or silver is on your line and you've got to go to work.

Both rainbows and silvers take to the air as soon as you
set the hook, and you sometimes think your heart will burst
before, finally, you find the fish at your feet, ready to be
released.

The variety of angling experiences available here are
impressive. A couple of anglers from California wanted a day
of dry-fly fishing—hard to find in August—but Chad flew
them to the headwaters of the Copper River, where they
hiked the upper river, catching lots of rainbows and gray-
ling—an extraordinarily beautiful fish that flies out of the
water, often taking your fly as it returns to the surface.

Another group flew to the Iliamna River and proclaimed it
the most beautiful setting in which they had ever fished—with
lots of rainbows to boot. This group said the Iliamna was their
favorite of all the rivers they fished that week—hard for me
to imagine after experiencing the Moraine, Ku, Gibraltar, and
Kamishak.

But then, one group chose to raft and fish the Gibraltar on
their final day, and reported it was the best rainbow fishing
they'd had—another surprise, because I liked the Moraine and
the Ku the best for rainbows.

One evening, Eric Wolf from Connecticut and I lugged a
canoe over a nearby beaver dam to fish one of the "pike lakes"
in back of the lodge. You can guess what species awaits eager
anglers in these waters.

Catching large northern pike on 8-weight rods, popping
mice on the surface of this wilderness pond, we were excited
beyond description. We fished until it was pitch black, and
then turned to discover we didn't know where we'd started
this adventure. The entire shoreline looked the same!

Eventually, we found the beaver dam and returned safely to the lodge, arriving about midnight. Of course, it remains light until after eleven P.M., giving relentless anglers more fishing opportunity after dinner. This was the only night I fished after dinner; every other evening we were too exhausted by the day's angling in these mighty rivers.

So here will be your dilemma in this angler's paradise: With so many species, so many big fish, and so many amazing rivers, when Chad asks, as he does after dinner every evening, "Where do you want to fish the next day?," what will you say? Believe me, that's the most stress you'll feel all week.

Home only a month, I already yearn to return to Alaska and Rainbow River Lodge. If you think you'd like to go next year, give me a call. I'd love to tell you more about this place and our trip and my love affair with Kami, Little Ku, and Moraine.

—September 1, 2004

Brook Trout Heaven

As an old brook trout fisherman, I can only hope Heaven is as good as this place. When death darkens my door, perhaps my eyes will suddenly open on the Leaf River, with only an eternity of fishing ahead. Hallelujah!

The fishing at this northern Quebec River is as good as it gets, with brook and lake trout, plus the bonus of an occasional Atlantic salmon.

Because I'm an outdoor writer, associated with a TV production company and a travel agency, and executive director of Maine's largest sportsmen's organization, I've been blessed with many free trips to Alaska, Montana, Quebec, and Labrador. In fact, I'd been to the Leaf in 2005 on a free trip to produce TV shows with Harry Vanderweide, host of *Northeast Journal*.

Normally I don't return to a place, because there are always new places available, for free. In fact, I've never paid for a fishing trip out of state before. But this year, I returned to the Leaf—and I paid for the trip. That's how much I love this river.

If trout fishing were an Olympic event, the Leaf River is where you'd hold it. This big river in the northern tundra is a world-class venue.

Let me tell you about one morning when we fished "the funnel," perhaps my favorite place on the river.

Our excellent and experienced guide, Serge, put us ashore about two hundred yards below this spot, where the river narrows sharply, a mountain of water rushing through and over huge boulders, quiet, deep pools of fish along the shore. I hiked to the top of the funnel, passing a complete set of caribou antlers, weathered on the shore right where the animal had dropped them.

The Leaf gives you a lot more than fish. Migrating caribou trot across the tundra, then swim the river—often right where you are fishing. One morning we saw a beautiful silver wolf, swimming across a very wide place in the river. We boated up to him for photos. What a thrill! Musk ox and even black bears are sometimes seen beside the river.

But of course, it's the fishing that brought me back, and this particular morning at the top of the funnel will tell you why. A ripple of water flowed about five feet from shore, and I casually cast a Muddler in brook trout colors. *Pow!* A huge trout burst through the surface and grabbed the fly.

The fight was on, and he took me well into the backing as my 5-weight rod had all the fish it could handle. When the trout was finally at my feet, I lifted it with my Boga-Grip to check the weight: a hefty three and a half pounds.

It is no exaggeration to say that the next seven casts caught seven trout between one and a half and three and a half pounds. They all rose to take the Muddler on the surface. Stepping upriver about twenty yards to check out the quiet pool at the top of this run, I gasped. Huge trout lay all over the pool.

Switching to a dry fly, a large Royal Wulff, I was astonished to see, as soon as it settled on the water, three gigantic trout rise to fight over it. That pool produced fifty trout for me in about two hours of heavenly angling, none smaller than one and a half pounds. Many were two and a half to three and a half pounds.

One was more memorable than the others. He looked big when he splashed to the surface to gobble my fly, and he took me downriver in the rapids very quickly, breaking my tippet and stealing my Royal Wulff, the only one in my fly box.

Forced to try other flies, I found a few that attracted these trout—but none as successful as the Royal Wulff. About a half-hour later, another huge trout rose to take a large Stimulator, and he too headed quickly into the rapids. But this time I skipped along the shore and kept up with him.

After a ten-minute battle, he was at my feet—the biggest trout I'd seen in this river—and I carefully photographed him lying in the water, then used the Boga-Grip to check his weight: four pounds!

While his weight and girth were surprising, the biggest surprise came when I grabbed the fly to remove it from his jaw. As my fingers reached for the fly, I stared at it in confusion. I was looking at my Royal Wulff—not the Stimulator I'd cast! It was the Royal Wulff that I'd lost about a half-hour earlier!

On one side of his jaw was my Royal Wulff, and on the other side, the Stimulator. This was the same fish I'd broken off earlier. I reattached the Wulff to my line and got back to catching trout on every cast.

One other fish in that pool was memorable. A large lake trout could be seen in the pool, and it chased the trout on my line quite often, sometimes grabbing my trout and fighting for them. Finally, I tied on a large green bass fly and tossed it into the current. On the first drift the laker grabbed it, and the fight was on. I landed him about ten minutes later. He weighed six pounds.

Although the Leaf is famous for its brookies—what they call "speckles"—the river also offers the challenge of lake trout, a tough, strong fish that will give you all the fight you can stand.

One day I broke off four big lakers. If you catch a smallish trout—two pounds on this river—oftentimes a laker will grab it and fight you for it.

I won't soon forget one of these lakers. He chased a small trout up to my feet, grabbed it before I could, and took off across the river as I struggled to stop him. About 150 yards out, he actually broke my line. He wasn't hooked; he just wouldn't let go of that brookie.

After landing six lakers, all ranging between six and seven pounds, and breaking off four larger lakers, I can tell you that some of your most remarkable fish will be lake trout.

Yes, There Are Salmon

I've never been an Atlantic salmon angler—too many casts required to catch too few fish. Too many fishless weeks. But the Leaf River holds salmon, and occasionally we'd spent time in specific pools trying to catch one.

We began my last day on the river in just such a pool— actually, several pools alongside a short but ferocious run of rapids. I'd picked up only a few brook trout in the upper pools and reached the final pool at the tail end of the rapids with vastly lowered expectations.

When I felt a tug on the line and picked it up, I knew I had a big fish, and I was thinking lake trout when the salmon leapt high out of the water. I shouted, and my fishing partner across the river, Herb Morse, says I was jumping up and down. I don't remember. Too excited.

After a twenty-minute fight and six breathtaking leaps, the six-pound, fresh-from-the-sea bright silver salmon lay where I'd placed him, in shallow, quiet water near shore. For ten minutes, I sat with him, as happy as an angler could hope to be, until he swam away to continue his journey home.

Now, I'm an Atlantic salmon angler.

A Walk along the River

I love to hike a river, searching for fish, and the Leaf offers the best hiking I've ever experienced. It's those isolated, unnoticed, unfished pools that can surprise you with memorable fish.

On a cold, blustery morning, I'd already hiked a caribou trail along the river for about two miles, fishing small pocket water and catching some real nice trout, when I gazed down at what I thought looked like an ideal pool: a ripple of water flowing over a cluster of large boulders, water about four feet deep.

I snuck down over the bank, took a position behind a large boulder, and carefully cast a Muddler about ten feet out. As it settled to the surface, there was a vicious splash as a large brookie grabbed it. He took me into my backing three times, and when finally brought to shore, he topped three pounds, a fish of beautiful colors.

I set him in quiet water to get his strength back, checked my fly and line, and cast to the same spot. *Bam!* Another big one. As I brought this trout into the quiet water, trout number one pulled out. This is how it went for about a half-hour.

When the guide called me to a delicious shore lunch (fish, of course), I'd hauled seven huge brook trout out of that small, boulder-strewn pool, all larger than two pounds, including one four-pound bruiser. One had taken my fly deep into his mouth, so he got to keep it; I cut it off rather than risk killing the trout to remove the fly.

After lunch in a quiet cove with a beautiful sandy beach, where we spotted fresh wolf tracks, I hustled back to the same pool. My dry fly caught one more three-pound trout. Then I switched to a heavy bass fly to catch two more very memorable fish—another four-pound brookie, and the tenth and final fish, a big surprise, a six-pound lake trout.

One pool, ten fish, two to six pounds—a lifetime memory—discovered on my morning walk along the Leaf River.

What I Like About the Leaf River

Experienced guides, large brook trout, strong lake trout, magnificent Atlantic salmon, a big, noisy river, walks along the shore searching for pools of trout, migrating caribou, a wolf swimming the river, lots of hearty food for breakfast and dinner, delicious shore lunches of potatoes and trout, jet boats skimming over huge, submerged boulders, barren rocky tundra as far as you can see, northern lights, comfortable cabins, hot showers, flush toilets—but most of all, the fish, and the river that holds them.

—August 2004

Duck Hunting Is a Love Affair with Nature

You may hear gunshots in the marsh this morning, as duck hunting opened thirty minutes before sunrise.

If things went according to plan, at six A.M. this morning I was seated in a comfortable chair under overhanging alders, my natural blind alongside Hopkins Stream, a panorama of feathered friends—decoys—spread out in front of me. Here's how I imagine the hunt will go.

As the sun touches the top of Bowen Hill to the east, black ducks settle into the marsh all around me. Can't shoot them until next week, though, so I squint left and right, hoping for mallards, or maybe some woodies.

The dog, a saw-grass Chesapeake Bay retriever appropriately named Blake Hill Buddy, Blake for short, is settled down beside me, also scanning the horizon for ducks, which he has dedicated his life to retrieving whenever his master is fortunate enough to knock one down.

We may see deer in the marsh, hear a cow moose calling somewhere in the woods behind us, witness a family of otter swim past, hissing at our decoys, admire beaver as they busy themselves on the opposite shore, watch a heron fish for his breakfast, all the while straining our eyes to the sky, left and right, hoping to spot a flock of ducks winging our way.

Duck hunting is a specialty sport nowadays. Less than ten thousand sportsmen hunt ducks in Maine today. It is an expensive sport. Hunting licenses are of course required, as well as a state duck stamp ($2.50) and a federal stamp ($15).

Steel shot is expensive, and the new, more-effective bismuth shot, just approved by federal authorities, costs even more.

Decoys don't come cheap these days, and camo clothing is also a necessity, enough for every type of weather. I've got camo T-shirts, camo flannel shirts, a camo hooded sweatshirt, camo pants, and camo hats. (No, I didn't buy camo under-wear.) Boots, foul-weather gear (camo, of course), and gloves complete the ensemble.

I forked over big bucks this year for an L.L. Bean all-weather Gore-Tex insulated camo coat, good enough to keep me warm during the second season, which goes into December locally, and into January for sea ducks on the coast. Yes, I conceded that the coat cost more than my wife's wedding dress, but I wear it more often, and you've got to factor in inflation over the past sixteen years that we've been married.

I am hoping we'll still be married after the duck season, although I swing almost immediately into deer season, and that's enough to strain any marriage. When the first duck season ends on October 14, I'll have just two weeks of scouting before the four weeks of the regular firearms season on deer begins, followed by (and I haven't dared tell my wife about this yet), a newly established two-week muzzle-loading season on deer. Fortunately, that ends before Christmas.

If I take up muzzle-loading, I'll need a new firearm, and that's another story. Bad enough what this duck hunting does to the pocketbook.

Along with the other stuff, a canoe is necessary, too, along with tote bags for all the gear and decoys, and duck calls, and the four-wheel-drive vehicle—absolutely necessary.

Okay. So what if I've invested about $35,000 so far, including this new camo folding chair in which I am comfortably ensconced as you read this column? It's a great sport. Worth every penny.

Conservationists are born in duck blinds. We put the resource first, reducing bag limits whenever necessary, putting up millions of dollars through Ducks Unlimited and other organizations to purchase and manage waterfowl habitat, constructing and caring for duck houses spread throughout the marshlands of Maine.

This year we'll bypass black ducks the first week so they can continue to rebuild their numbers. We'll have no goose season at all, as those magnificent birds struggle to overcome a serious nesting problem experienced in 1992, in the Ungava Bay region of Canada.

But we'll be out there, no matter what the weather, because we love ducks, and duck hunting. What's not to love?

Imagine yourself this morning, seated alongside me on Hopkins Stream. Hardwood trees sporting glorious red and yellow leaves reflect in the water and stand guard along both sides of the stream. The setting is gorgeous.

About seven A.M. we'll enjoy Lin's cranberry muffins and piping hot coffee. We may canoe upstream to see what we can see. There will be lots of wildlife, and plenty of peace and quiet, too. We'll converse with the dog. And we'll see a lot of ducks.

Tonight, we'll roast a couple if we are lucky today. Actually, we are lucky, regardless of whether or not we bag our supper.

We're in the marsh this morning. Perhaps you heard us.

—*Kennebec Journal* (October 2, 1995)

The Privilege of Deer Hunting

As the canoe slid quietly along Hopkins Stream in the pre-dawn darkness, eleven-year-old son Joshua jumped when an unseen beaver slapped the water right beside him. "Wow, what was that, Dad?" he asked, more exclamation than question.

It was the opening morning of the firearms season on deer, and this would be a family affair, with my dad already in his new tree stand in a nearby woodlot, and Josh and I taking our places in a streamside blind. As the sun hit the tops of the trees across the stream, I shivered from the cold and the exciting anticipation of another November spent pursuing Maine's most magnificent and wily game animal, the white-tailed deer.

After an hour in the blind, Josh and I snuck downstream, darting from bush to bush, until we spied two deer feeding on cranberries. We crept to within a hundred yards after verifying, through my scope, that they were a doe and lamb, both off limits to this buck hunter.

After scaring them off, Josh got down to business, picking cranberries, and I discovered a set of bones belonging to a small animal. We packed up the berries and bones (not in the same bag), canoed across the stream, and hunted our way to Dad's stand.

Arriving there a bit later than anticipated (after all, we'd had a lot of excitement down on the stream), we rushed to Manchester to the fabulous hunters' breakfast sponsored by the Lions Club. By the time we pushed away from the table, I felt quite contented—and eager to get back into the woods. Dad and Josh went on to other activities, and I hiked back downstream, found a nice soft pine grove, and had a nap. As far as I know, no deer came by while I slept.

The doe was in front of me before I ever heard a sound. She moved gracefully and quickly along, but with great caution, fully aware of her surroundings. But she didn't see me and I hunkered down, glad that I was downwind, because deer have a terrific sense of smell. She moved toward the beaver bog, a huge open area to my left, but stopped sharply behind a fir thicket, then dashed back over the small rise to my right.

A minute later she was back with the same routine, moving to the edge of the bog, stopping behind the fir thicket, then spooking and dashing back over the rise. Three minutes later she did it all again, and when I finally moved toward home in order to do a scheduled radio interview at ten A.M., the doe was still hovering close by, refusing to leave the area. I presumed she had a date with a buck, and cursed my bad luck at having to leave.

By the time I returned, the buck had visited, tearing up the turf, shredding small cedars with his antlers, and generally leaving the place a mess. I'll be sitting there some afternoon this week, hoping for his return.

The next afternoon, however, I selected a favorite tree stand on the edge of my woodlot. Enjoying a nice afternoon, a large crack out of the clear-cut in front of my stand focused my attention on the approach of a huge bull moose with a magnificent rack. When he got to the edge of the woods where I sat in my tree stand, he seemed to recognize that I was something unusual, and he sauntered right up to me, stood about twenty feet away, and looked up.

I was awfully glad I'd put the stand up so high, well out of his reach. He moseyed around the stand for an hour, at one time standing in a sunny spot for fifteen minutes while the previous night's rain steamed off his body. He was actually in a vapor cloud part of the time, a very strange sight indeed.

It wasn't until I got out of my stand (cautiously) and spoke to him that he trotted off toward the stream. I took the tote road in the other direction.

Much of my time is spent scouring for bucks, locating key ground scrapes to stand watch over, and meandering through the woods, one or two steps at a time, watching, listening, looking for any telltale parts of a white-tailed deer.

You see a lot at this slow pace: the pileated woodpecker which swoops through the trees, a great horned owl which alights nearby and gives you a scary stare, the tiny ermine that darts along in his winter coat of white, a rabbit that quivers in fright at your approach and then hops off when he decides the game is up, a frog gamely trying to get up a steep incline.

This is deer hunting in Maine. And I feel privileged to experience it again this month.

—*Kennebec Journal* (November 8, 1993)

Passing On the Hunting Tradition

Thursday's Thanksgiving traditions have always focused on the family for us. I can remember Thanksgiving dinners in the basement of my great-aunt Flora and uncle Johnny Mitchell's Bowdoin Street home in Winthrop, long folding tables snaking this way and that, heaped with food, surrounded by laughter and love.

Mmmm . . . I can taste the turkey now, the stuffing, mashed potatoes laden with gravy, succulent squash. And oh, those pies for dessert.

Thanksgiving isn't the only time that family traditions are important. For Christmas, Aunt Flora always provided the best homemade donuts for breakfast at the Smith house. That tradition is still alive. Flora's daughter, Delora Farrington, now cooks and delivers the donuts. Brother Gordon and I have been known to scarf down an unmentionably large number of them on Christmas morn.

Another important tradition has been handed down this year in my family. I was born a Maine sportsman, raised a Maine sportsman, and will die a Maine sportsman. Dad made sure of the first two. My love for the Maine woods ensures the latter. And this year, Grampy Smith and I have been joined in those wonderful woods by son Joshua, hunting seriously for the first time at age fifteen. It's been a very special hunting season for us.

Josh found Dad's deer for him after he shot a spike horn on opening day. Josh was sitting beside me when I shot my six-point, 150-pound buck the following Friday. Somehow the torch was passed as he paddled me out to retrieve my buck from Moose Pond, where it had expired. He seemed to be in charge, spotting the buck in the water, directing us to shore, suggesting a way to get the buck into the canoe.

When did he get so smart? And so tall? Did it all happen this year? I think I'll remember it that way, although this treat must have been baking for many years. And I was with Josh when he got in some shooting of his own about a week ago at another nice buck. He missed, but that's also part of hunting.

It's not just the shooting I'll remember from this season. What has also been memorable is this: selecting a new rifle for Josh, along with a good-quality scope with some expert advice from the outfitters; shooting it at a local gravel pit and on our woodlot as we prepared for opening day; Josh and I taking an afternoon to scout the area and build a blind on top of a large boulder, just off a well-traveled deer trail; seeing a deer from that blind on the first morning I sat there and letting it escape, hoping it would return someday when Josh was sitting there.

I'll remember tracking a big buck and a pair of does in the snow last Saturday with Josh, and the disappointment on Josh's face when all of the tracks led to the edge of Hopkins Stream and out into the water. They'd escaped to the other side.

"That's deer hunting," explained the sage. "If it was easy, it wouldn't be half as much fun."

I'm not sure Josh agreed. But he's got to pay his dues. I've missed deer every way imaginable, made every mistake a hunter can make, stood sentry along deer tails through the coldest November days without seeing a thing, shot through trees, jammed my rifle with a big buck standing there and staring at me before wandering off with a smile on its face.

But oh, it's great to be out there. And Josh is catching the spirit. His face is intent as we search the edge of the bog for movement. The sound of a sharp *crack* brings his head up, and he surveys the woods, hoping to see a whitetail sneaking along.

I watch him in wonder. He is me, thirty-three years ago, sitting on a ridge out back of Dad's old farm in North Wayne. I'm sort of lackadaisical in my deer stand now. I do a lot of reading. Not Josh. He's watching every moment, ready for his deer to step out.

He notes birds, squirrels, the tracks of other animals in the snow. We spot a fisher's tracks on Saturday, maybe the one that's been eating cats in our neighborhood. Hope the trapper gets that one.

Finally, chowing down on venison burgers last weekend, listening to Josh rave about the great taste, trying to convince his mother and sister to try it, telling them they'd never be able to tell the difference between their beef burgers and our venison burgers, I knew he was hooked.

Where once my pool table was half-covered with fluorescent orange hats, coats, gloves, deer scents and calls, rattling antlers, knives, guns, and bullets, now it is completely covered. For we have two hunters in the house now. It's our tradition.

—*Kennebec Journal* (November 24, 1997)

Update: Josh shot his deer the next year. Alas, it was his last. For better employment opportunities, he left Maine for Massachusetts, and has little time and no place to hunt. He does get to Maine to fish, though; I cling to that. And now I'm working on my grandsons.

Reflections on Maine Fishing

They follow state hatchery trucks, eager to catch those fat brook trout stocked this month all over the state. They crowd roadsides, casting from bridges. They troll the shores of lakes and ponds, hoping to catch a landlocked salmon.

Some seek a feed of tasty perch; others dream of a huge northern pike. Many focus on bass, Maine's most popular fish. Twice as many bass are caught every year than brook trout. An angler army is out this week on the brooks, streams, rivers, ponds, and lakes. But the troops are depleted, and we're losing our recreational fishing economy.

Maine falls far short of its potential when it comes to inland and coastal recreational fishing. We lack investment, management, infrastructure including water access, and marketing.

Between 1995 and 2003, we lost 30,000 nonresident anglers, a 28 percent loss, representing an economic hit of $20 million or more. Sales of fishing licenses to nonresidents peaked in 1989 at 108,698. But this problem is not limited to nonresidents. Mainers have given up fishing here as well. Sales of fishing licenses to residents peaked in 1991 at 203,245. Total fishing license sales peaked in 1990 at 310,278. Last year we were down more than 50,000 licenses since that peak year.

Ironically, to address our current budget problems, the governor proposed that the Department of Inland Fisheries and Wildlife (DIF&W) eliminate its only marketing position, stop attending out-of-state sportsmen's shows, postpone publications of important fishing brochures and other information, and, unbelievably, stop providing fishing rule books. The

118

legislature's Fish and Wildlife and Appropriations committees have reversed most of those decisions.

Recreational fishing contributes significantly to our economy. The 2006 National Survey of Fishing, Hunting, and Wildlife-Associated Recreation reported that $257,124,000 was spent in Maine by anglers. Nonresidents spent $124,812,000. This includes both fresh- and saltwater angling.

But we could be doing so much better. The federal survey reported 10,000 more nonresidents fished freshwater in New Hampshire than Maine in 2006! And 25,000 more nonresidents fished in Montana than Maine.

With more investment, better management, and stronger marketing, recreational fishing could deliver a lot more to our economy. This matters to many Mainers, from the two guys at Kennebec Lures who make fishing lures in their Sanford garage, to the locally owned fly shop, to the retired warden who ties and sells flies in the North Country, to the guides and sporting camps all over the state. Let's examine one part of this equation: stocked fish.

In 2008, DIF&W stocked 1.3 million fish totaling 360,000 pounds. In 1996, Colorado's Division of Wildlife stocked more than 65 million warm-water fish and 14.6 million cold-water fish, including 4.8 million catchable-sized rainbow trout. Guess where people go to fish these days?

A Hatchery Commission was established in 1999 to assess and evaluate Maine's recreational fish production facilities and set production goals at state-owned facilities. The Hatchery Commission recommended fish production goals of 1,958,063 fish weighing 865,077 pounds by 2012. In 2008 we fell 658,000 fish and 505,000 pounds short of our goal.

Then there is the problem of access. Maine is blessed with a lot of public water, about a million acres in nearly 2,000 lakes and ponds, 32,000 miles of rivers, brooks, and streams, and over 3,000 miles of coastline. While the state ranks only thirty-ninth among states in land area, it ranks ninth in total water area, not counting small water bodies. It places fourth in miles of tidal shoreline, fourth in lake acreage, and eleventh in river miles.

The value of this resource goes well beyond these statistics. Few states have water resources of the quality found in Maine. I've often said that Maine's rivers are the arteries in our economic body. Yet our legal access to this abundance of water is very limited. There are hundreds of lakes and ponds without any legal public access, and the places where we do have access are not always well known.

And Mainers have no legal access to moving water. We have walk-in access rights to Great Ponds, and that's it. We have no legal access to brooks, streams, and rivers. Adjacent landowners own the land under our rivers, brooks, and streams, and can prevent us from standing in those waters.

The Maine legislature has addressed some of these problems this session, and DIF&W and the group for which I toil, the Sportsman's Alliance of Maine, are working together to improve fishing in our state. You can help. Go fish.

—Central Maine Newspapers (May 6, 2009)

Gene Letourneau's Last Cast

The warm breeze wafting through Sacred Heart Church in Waterville last Thursday surely must have carried Gene Letourneau's spirit to the great hunting ground beyond our imagination.

As expected, Letourneau's funeral featured stories about fly fishing and hunting dogs, but we also heard about his musical talent, faith in God, and devotion to his family, especially his lovely wife Lou, who died in 1996. The light went out for Gene then, and he began his own hike to join Lou. He's there now, sipping that heavenly cold, clear springwater.

We are bereft, for the irreplaceable outdoor writer has left behind his canoe without so much as a wake we can ride for even a short way. His paddle dipped too quietly, I guess, for his bosses to realize the impact he was having on the people of Maine, his devoted readers and correspondents.

Gene's daily outdoors column, titled "Sportsmen Say," that started my day as a kid, is gone, found in none of today's daily newspapers, still wondering why they're losing subscribers.

I was privileged to appear in a video of reverence and praise presented to Gene at his spectacular retirement party at the Augusta Civic Center a few years ago. My remarks focused on the real magic of his newspaper column, in the section called "Chips from the Blazed Trail."

It was here that Gene presented firsthand reports he received in letters and phone calls from sportsmen throughout the state, accounts of their exciting adventures, latest fishing successes, hunting prowess, or simple observations of wild birds and animals. I always felt this was the secret of his column: He let the voices of his readers and fans be heard. "Sportsmen Say," indeed.

Gene connected with people, whether or not they shared his passion for hunting and fishing, because he presented Maine's outdoor traditions in their own words, kept them informed, shared his extensive knowledge (while keeping some secret ponds to himself to protect those precious resources), always in simple, clear prose.

Every day started for us with some exciting news from Gene. Even cooped up in the office, we could be transported, briefly, into the wilds of Maine. It was glorious. And it came to us every day.

Gene was the only reporter, in all the years I've lobbied at the legislature and attended hearings there, to be called upon by legislators to offer his views from the audience. "Gene, what do you think?" they'd often ask in the middle of a hearing or work session. And he would, in his humble, quiet voice, without rising from his chair in the back, tell them.

That would be unthinkable today, a reporter called upon at a public hearing to provide advice. Such was the respect we all felt for this remarkable man.

Not surprisingly, his advice cut to the quick, offering common sense and focusing on what was right for the natural resources he cherished. He made it seem simple. And it is.

Gene often criticized the Department of Inland Fisheries and Wildlife, holding their feet to the fire for mistakes. And he saw many. He was especially harsh on the agency for spending all of its federal funds on research and staff instead of habitat purchases and protection. First to recognize the arrival of coyotes and their horrible impact on deer, he waited impatiently for years for DIF&W to acknowledge their presence, and later, their impact.

I was doing well at Gene's beautiful funeral service until his son, Fred, cast this final poem upon the water Gene now paddles.

At this time in my life, I can see the trail ends.
I've caught more than my limit of good times and friends.
I thank God every day for a long happy life,
For the music we made, for the love of my wife.
I'll take down the canoe for one final trip,
And cast a Grey Ghost gently over the slip.
Let no one believe that the best days are through,
Inscribe on my stone, please, "Gone fishin' with Lou."

I cast a few tears for that final trip we all must take, that final cast we all can take, and for what we have lost already. It seems impossible that we will ever again pick up a daily newspaper in Maine to read about the hunting and fishing adventures of a favorite writer and our friends and fellow sportsmen. We get occasional reports, usually in weekend papers, but nothing day in and day out.

Maine's daily newspapers are sailing on different water today. I guess they figure the quiet waters canoed by Gene Letourneau are no longer exciting enough to sell papers. Oh, how wrong they are.

There was a lot of passion in that quiet, humble man, a sparkle in his eyes that let you know he loved every bit of his life, every song, every minute in the field. His was an exciting life, shared every day with his readers.

Hundreds of thousands of Mainers revered Gene Letourneau and doted on his every word. Where, oh where, will we find that daily dose of outdoor Maine now?

—*Kennebec Journal* (July 13, 1998)

Nothing Finer than Family Fishing

As I cast a Brown Wulff to a Sourdnahunk Lake brook trout
that had risen about forty feet from the boat, I was startled by
a shout from young Joshua at the other end of the boat.

"I got him!" he exclaimed. The water about six feet in front
of me erupted as Josh's brookie fought to separate himself
from my son's Hornberg. Josh had spotted the trout's rise right
beside the boat while my eyes were looking much farther out,
and he had carefully dropped his own fly into the middle of
the ring.

The fish struck immediately, and Josh professionally set the
hook. Up went his rod just as we had practiced, and the battle
was on. Keeping a tight line, Josh played the fish well, bringing it in quickly so as not to tire it needlessly if we decided to
release it.

But I took one look at that brookie boatside and knew it was
a keeper. Josh has released his share of fish and he deserved
this one. I dropped it out of the net into the bottom of the
boat and almost in unison our two voices said, "Wow, what a
fish!"

It was Josh's biggest fish to date, a colorful and fat thirteen-
inch brook trout. It perfectly matched a fish I'd caught earlier
that evening, and we limited our catch to those two fish,
releasing the rest that evening.

If there's a bigger thrill for a twelve-year-old than casting a
dry fly and catching a hefty thirteen-inch native brook trout
in the shadow of Mount Katahdin, I guess I don't know what

it is. Heck, it's a pretty big thrill for me, watching my son working that rod and bringing in that trout.

I'm doubly blessed because my nine-year-old daughter is an avid angler too. Earlier that week, Hilary joined Josh in a small boat they paddle around a nearby beaver pond. Josh fashioned a rod for her from a nearby alder branch and attached about six feet of thread to it, at the end of which he tied on a small dry fly, part of his collection of old flies that his grandfather had purchased for him at a yard sale.

Hilary didn't hook any trout in the pond with that rod, but she hooked herself on fly fishing. After that, I couldn't keep her out of the boat! And she adored her alder-branch rod.

A day later we traveled to a nearby brook with our respective fly rods. We scampered from the Baxter Park perimeter road down a steep bank to the brook's edge where I waded the stream, carrying Hilary on my back to the other side.

Eventually I placed her, still fishing her alder branch with thread and dry fly, in the middle of the brook, perched on a downed tree, so she could fish a deep hole that I was certain held some trout.

She began getting strikes immediately and fished intently for over an hour, trying to hook those tiny trout, none of which go more than six inches. She never hooked one, but she got more strikes with that foolish alder branch than I did with my $150 L.L. Bean fly rod.

Later that week, Josh and I fished the evening mayfly hatch in a stiff wind, very few trout rising, and even fewer taking an interest in our dry flies. I tried a parcel of flies from grasshopper imitations to the ever-faithful Brown Wulff, with no luck.

Shortly before dark, Josh cast his Hornberg about fifteen feet toward shore, watched it ride on the waves for about a minute, keeping his line tight. *Smash!* A trout pounded his fly and he brought the rod up to set the hook, cool and calm.

It was a handsome twelve-inch trout and we kept it, our only fish of the night. After I continued to cast for about twenty minutes, frustrated with my own lack of action, I looked at Josh and he said, very seriously, "Dad, why don't you try my rod. I've got all the fish I want."

Boy, talk about being humbled. I thanked him, thanked God for him, and told him to keep fishing. We both had all the fish we wanted.

On the Fourth of July, the Smith family enjoyed a feast of three poached trout, two of which were contributed by the twelve-year-old. I can't remember a finer meal, and it had nothing to do with the food.

—*Kennebec Journal* (1994)

A Change in Streams, Trout, and Fishing Techniques

To a twelve-year-old boy, it was wilderness, a place of fantasy, escape, high adventure. The wilderness was only a short half-mile walk from his house to the very top of High Street, into a tote road through a forest of sugar maples, huge oaks, and fir thickets, over the hill and into the next valley.

He'd seen bobcat, deer, partridge, and lots of squirrels there, but it was along the small brook that meandered through the forested valley that he spent most of his time. That cold, sheltered brook held wild trout, many trout, colorful trout, huge six- and seven-inch trout. He dreamed of them often.

But the reality was even better than his dreams. Nestled in his backpack along with peanut butter and jelly sandwiches and candy bars, the boy carried a can of worms, usually dug from his 4-H Award–winning garden out back of the house. Sometimes the can was brimming with huge night crawlers gently pulled from their holes on the front lawn during an evening rainstorm when his parents allowed the boy to stay up late in order to replenish his crawler supply.

Sneaking across the lawn with a flashlight, quick reaction and fast hands were required to grab the crawlers, only partly out of their holes, and gentle hands to coax them all the way out of the ground without ripping them apart. The boy was an expert. Sometimes he did so well on a rainy night that he could sell his surplus to other fishermen, friends of his dad. They used the crawlers to catch perch in Maranacook Lake.

He never told them about the trout in the brook up over the hill. Even then, he had an innate sense that too many fishermen could spoil a good thing. But he did take his buddies along sometimes, and they'd make a daylong adventure out of it.

His fishing gear was basic stuff. The boy had an old rod hardly longer than himself and a small spinning reel, something his dad had discarded. A plain bare hook was tied onto the end of strong monofilament line, line hefty enough that he never lost a hook to bottom. Ever. Which was a good thing, because he only had a couple of hooks.

His fishing technique was simple too. Sneak along the alders, poke the rod out over the brook just above those places where he knew a trout would be hiding, dip the hook with a gob of worms into the water, let it drift past the hiding place, and when the trout darted out, give the rod a sharp yank, which hooked the fish and pulled it right out of the water and onto the bank, all in one motion.

The boy knew his water, every riffle, deep pool, long bank. He didn't know this was called *reading the water*. He just knew where those trout lived. And he got to be an exceptional trout fisherman. Returning home on late afternoons with a creel—really just an old canvas bag he'd found in the barn—full of ten six- and seven-inch trout—well, that was the finest kind of living for a twelve-year-old boy.

He'd clean the trout after he got home and his mom would fry them up in cornmeal in a huge, old cast-iron skillet for supper, with lots of praise for her little sportsman who could feed his family. And boy, did those trout taste great. For the rest of his life there'd be no finer meal than wild brook trout, fried.

Of course things change, even deep, cold, fast-rushing brooks, and when the boy returned to town after college to settle into the banking profession and trudged one Saturday morning up to the end of High Street, he was surprised to find that the street had been extended deep into his wilderness. Much of the forest was gone, and the last half-mile of the brook he had fished so many times now flowed through a housing development.

He fished the entire length of the brook that day and caught only four trout, all less than six inches long. You can't go back, even to fish.

So the boy moved on, buying a twelve-foot boat to troll the lakes for brown trout that were introduced to a lot of Maine waters that could no longer grow brook trout because of diminished water quality. Some thought the trout were lost when water in the small tributaries which fed the lakes was warmed by timber harvesting and development along their banks. Those tributaries had been trout factories in the old days. The young man thought about that, content to gas up the boat and troll for hours up and down the lake.

Sometimes he'd hit the ocean for a cooler full of mackerel taken on Christmas-tree rigs six at a time as he and his dad trolled Johns Bay in Pemaquid. Lots of fun. Nothing like taking six fish at a time.

He clung to his worms too, filling up buckets with white perch during their spring spawning run and taking stringers of huge bass off their spawning beds in late May and early June with those old, reliable night crawlers.

Marriage and children intruded, reducing fishing time, but before he knew it, the kids were old enough to fish. He took them perch fishing. Soon they could fling a worm and bobber out there with the best of them. A feast of fried perch wasn't hard to take either. But the kids never fished on their own. "Kids these days have too many things to do," he often said.

Occasionally, he daydreamed about that wilderness trout stream up over High Street, but that only made him sad, so he stopped thinking about it.

He progressed in his profession, started his own consulting business, and soon had amassed enough savings to think about buying a camp someplace up north in the real wilderness. More and more he found himself thinking about the old brook, those colorful trout, wilderness adventures.

His boy was ten years old and his girl was seven when the perfect camp was found on Sourdnahunk Lake, just outside the northwest corner of Baxter Park, a forever-wild sanctuary of forty-six mountains, dozens of small ponds, and miles of mountain streams. And oh yes, lots of wild brook trout.

Just one problem: Almost all of the waters were fly-fishing-only. He'd read a bit about fly fishing but never tried it.

But the camp was perfect, the setting sublime, and they bought it in September as the brookies began to spawn. Oh, how beautiful those fish were—and how difficult to catch.

With a borrowed fly rod and a few Royal Coachman flies, he flayed the water in great frustration. And caught just one trout all month. But it was gorgeous, thirteen inches long and very tasty.

One month, one fish, but he was hooked on fly fishing.

The next spring, before going to camp, he attended L.L. Bean's introductory fly-fishing school, a three-day adventure, after which he headed to Sourdnahunk with much more enthusiasm—and an improved casting motion—and of course, with a lot more gear.

The new 8-weight rod and a world-class collection of flies also helped. He caught a few fish, enough to feed the family a supper of fried trout several times in May and June. Yummy.

His boy began joining him at times, spending his time practicing casting with an old fly rod which his Grampy had purchased at a yard sale and left at camp. Even Grampy was trying this new fly-fishing thing.

But what really caught his attention was the daughter, casting from shore using an alder branch and string that her brother had rigged up for her. She was amazing to watch. She really had the motion and rhythm down pat. Her little arm made a compact cast which was stunning in its simplicity and effectiveness.

One afternoon he took the kids to a nearby trout stream where worms were allowed and they limited out. But something didn't feel right. The trout were tiny, barely legal at six inches. *Didn't fish that size used to thrill me?* he wondered.

So the next time they tried the trout stream, they took the fly rods and did just as well. And because they'd eaten their fill of trout by that time, they released every single trout. It felt kind of good. As they trudged down the stream on their way out, a deer stepped into the water about fifty feet away and began drinking. When they got back to camp there were plenty of stories to tell. The empty creel didn't seem all that important.

And finally one evening as they enjoyed a stunning sunset while casting to rising trout on the lake, his son finally hit a ring and caught a trout, an eleven-inch beauty, his very first fish with a fly rod. Keeping his rod tip high, he handled it like a pro, bringing it quickly to the side of the boat. But when the father reached out to lift the fish into the boat, he heard his son say, "Dad, we don't need that one. Can we let it go?"

The boy's first big trout on a fly rod. And he wanted to let it go. The father couldn't believe it, and tried briefly to talk his son into keeping the fish, but the boy persisted. Lifting the fish gently from the water, the father twisted the fly out of the trout's mouth and gently released it back into the water.

After that the father started to admire the boy's casts. Somehow, quite suddenly, the boy was hitting every ring. And the father was busy releasing trout, almost too busy to fish himself. The next time the father did manage to catch a fish, he heard the boy say again, "Dad, we don't need that one. Let it go."

Oh, it was hard. Catch-and-release was not his heritage. Trout in the creel was how he judged his success. It just didn't seem right to let a keeper go. But for the boy's sake, the father began releasing fish that evening.

Eventually, with both his son and daughter releasing nearly all their fish, the father caught the spirit. Now they measured their success by how many fish they released. Two or three suppers a summer of fried trout were sufficient. The rest went back into the lake.

He started thinking about that boyhood stream and all the fish he'd taken out of it. Could he have ruined it, before the developers ever arrived?

When his daughter was nine she could cast a beautiful line, so he bought her a seven-and-a-half-foot, 4-weight rod. (Okay, so he planned to use it himself, too, on some of those small alder-choked streams.) The boy was twelve and tying flies by then, and had become nearly a fanatic about fly fishing. He'd gotten a nice eight-and-a-half-foot, 7-weight rod for Christmas.

The father could still outfish the boy most of the time. Then one evening, when he had taken the boat out alone for the last half-hour of fishing after the sun had set, to catch one fish for his morning's breakfast, it happened.

The biggest trout of the evening was just ten inches long, a bit disappointing in a lake that held lots of thirteen- and fourteen-inch fish. But he kept it and returned to camp. Stepping onto the camp's porch, he heard the boy exclaim, "Dad, wait till you see my fish!"

Leading the father to the cooler on the porch, the boy shined his flashlight on a monstrous trout, a sixteen-inch beauty, the largest ever caught by the family here at camp. The boy had cast from shore shortly after sunset and landed the huge trout.

"Gee, Dad, what's that puny fish you've got in your hand there?" laughed the boy.

He ignored the barb. Looking longingly at his boy's trout, he replied, "Son, that is a fantastic fish."

It was the only fish the boy kept all summer.

So it was that a twelve-year-old boy fishing a stream near home with worms, and filling his creel nearly every time with six-inch brook trout, turned into a different twelve-year-old boy casting flies to eager wild brookies on a northern pond and keeping only a single fish all summer long.

Of Brookies and Bass and Grandsons

The fourteen-inch wild native brook trout took the first dry fly offered when I arrived at my favorite pool about a mile from the road in this cold, free-flowing North Woods stream. The trout's stunning spawning colors erased any doubt that there is a God.

In recent years, Maine has stepped up protection of its native brookies, important when you understand that this state has 97 percent of all the remaining native brook trout in the United States.

Wading downstream to my favorite pool, holding hundreds of spawning trout (I caught more than fifty in two hours), I'd been forced out of the stream at one point when three large river otters let me know they disliked my presence. They were more aggressive than the cow moose and calf I'd walked around at the point I entered the stream.

Not long before I'd driven to camp to enjoy this fall fishing experience, I'd taken my grandson to a favorite pond near my Mount Vernon home, just twenty miles from the State Capitol, to fish for smallmouth bass.

Six-year-old Addison sat in the front seat of the old aluminum canoe and cast a jig toward shore, working it back as skillfully as a professional bass angler, while his grandfather watched with a mixture of love, pride, and anticipation.

There! An eager bass grabbed the jig, Addi lifted the rod, the fish was on, the fish was up and out of the water!

"That's a huge fish, Addison!" I exclaimed. And his smile told me that the public purchase of the land surrounding this pond in the Kennebec Highlands was a very wise decision.

Maine added two million acres in the last decade to its public lands inventory to make sure all of us have access to this state's amazing natural resources. As a river angler, I've been blessed to fish magnificent rivers from Alaska and Montana to Quebec and Labrador. Maine's rivers are equally spectacular.

In July, I slipped my kayak into the Kennebec River just fifteen miles above the capital city of Augusta. The forty-seven smallmouth bass caught that morning were memorable, as were the two dozen bald eagles along the river. Most astonishing—I didn't see another person! And this section of the river is so undeveloped you'd think you were in the Alaskan bush.

Waters all over the state draw my attention year-round, yet I remain true to my roots. Nothing pleases me more than a day on a small brook, catching brook trout. My first fishing experiences involved dunking worms into tiny brooks. Today I prefer to cast flies.

My favorite brook regularly gives up as many as a hundred brookies in a half-day of fishing. Except for that day I waded a mile down the brook and got mixed up with a pair of mating bears. That called for a hasty retreat!

No need to retreat if you're thinking of fishing here.

—*Maine Invites You,* Maine Tourism Association 2012 Guidebook

It's Time to Get the Lead Out

Linda and I were working in the garden when we heard a voice hollering from the woods. I thought I heard, "I've got a loon, and need help!" That didn't make a lot of sense to me, but sure enough, when I stepped into the woods, there was Shearon Murphy with a loon cradled under her arm. And here is that loon's story.

Jane Naliboff photographed the loon the morning of September 7 on Minnehonk Lake. When she got home and loaded the photos into her computer, something looked very wrong. So she e-mailed the photos to Keel Kemper, a wildlife biologist with Maine's Department of Inland Fisheries and Wildlife.

Keel agreed that something was wrong with the loon, and recommended a rescue. Jane contacted Avian Haven, and late that afternoon, Shearon Murphy, a volunteer waterfowl rescuer, showed up with her kayak, paddled out to the loon, now in the outlet of the lake right behind our Mount Vernon home, and simply reached down and picked up the bird. Definitely not something that would ever happen with a healthy loon.

Looking into the right eye of that beautiful creature, I too knew that something was very wrong. The loon's head and neck languished on Shearon's hip as I drove her back to her vehicle, where Jane met us, along with Barbara Skapa, who had joined in the rescue mission.

We loaded the loon into a box, covered it up with a sheet I'd grabbed from our garage, and Shearon took off to deliver the bird to Avian Haven, where a large lead sinker was found in its gizzard.

The next day, Jane published her story and lots of photos in the *Daily Bulldog*, reporting, "The good news is that after lavage [pouring water into the gizzard to flush out the sinker], it worked. The sinker came out! [The loon is] now getting chelation therapy to lower the lead level to a normal range. When that happens, it will be released back to its natural environment. It's a happy ending for what was almost another dead waterbird due to human behavior."

Boy, I was some old happy to read this, and pleased with the small role I'd played in the rescue of this beautiful creature.

Alas, at nine P.M. that night, Jane posted this: "It is with great sadness and disappointment that I must tell you: Despite a successful lavage procedure, our friend survived only a few more hours before succumbing to lead poisoning. Everyone did all they could, and we are all heartbroken."

The rest of the story is even worse. Quite a few years ago, Maine Audubon proposed and lobbied for a new law banning the sale of lead sinkers weighing one ounce or less.

On behalf of the Sportsman's Alliance of Maine, I successfully lobbied to reduce the weight to half an ounce or less, and the bill was enacted. It is illegal today in Maine to sell lead sinkers of one-half ounce or less.

The lead sinker that killed the loon that's the subject of this story weighed five-eighths of an ounce—slightly more than the half-ounce that was banned. I was stunned to hear this from the owner of Avian Haven. And humbled, feeling partially responsible for the death.

At the time Audubon proposed the bill, alternatives to lead sinkers were new to the market, and much more expensive. That was my rationale for opposing the bill and working to reduce the weight of the banned sinkers.

But the weight reduction was not the only error made. We didn't ban the use of lead sinkers.

Even though lots of alternatives are readily available today for lead sinkers; prices of those other types of sinkers have come down; and stores, including L.L. Bean, don't sell lead sinkers anymore, many anglers continue to use lead sinkers. Although I rarely use sinkers these days, my tackle boxes are full of lead sinkers—enough for at least my next two generations of anglers.

Soon after that loon died, I collected all those sinkers and set them aside. But when I inquired about disposal, I discovered that it wouldn't be easy. Lead sinkers are hazardous waste. That's right; we're fishing with hazardous waste!

I'll be working with my local transfer station supervisor to properly dispose of my lead sinkers. And I urge all Maine anglers to join me in ridding our tackle boxes of lead sinkers. Better late than never.

—Central Maine Newspapers (2012)

Update: In 2013 the Maine legislature banned the use and sale of lead sinkers of one ounce or less. I testified in favor of the bill, which was proposed by Maine Audubon. Perhaps there will be forgiveness in Heaven if we admit our mistakes before we get there.

Birding Gems

Not far from Monica's Chocolates in Lubec, my compass point, and tucked up behind the water-treatment plant, Linda and I discovered one of hundreds of special places in Maine that have been purchased by conservation interests.

This one was a surprise. We were taking a driving tour of the south end of town and pulled into the treatment plant parking lot to turn around when we saw the QUODDY TRAILS sign. Turns out this was purchased for you and me by our Land for Maine's Future program. The boardwalk led to a huge sandbar and beach and then meandered through the adjacent wetland.

We'd set out that morning from our rental cabin at Island Chalet on Campobello Island, a bit of Canadian paradise, to explore the Boot Head Preserve's birding trail suggested in Bob Duchesne's *Maine Birding Trail* guidebook. We were delayed in getting to Boot Head by all the birds behind the water-treatment plant. The previous week we'd been birding on another spectacular trail in our Kennebec County backyard.

The Mountain Trail just north of Belgrade Village on Route 27 is the first parcel acquired by the Belgrade Regional Conservation Alliance as it began to accumulate, with help from the Land for Maine's Future and other funding sources, the magnificent 6,000-acre Kennebec Highlands. This trail is scenic, has lots of birds, and is easy walking. We'd selected it because Duchesne's book reported scarlet tanagers here, and we'd seen none this year. Two hundred yards up the trail, there they were.

Maine's conservation lands are playing an increasing role in my life, for several reasons. First, they're some of the most spectacular places in our state. Second, many have trails and other infrastructure (such as easy access to water). Third, access to private land is becoming more difficult and contentious and now requires, in many places, that we obtain permission before entering or using the land. Much of Maine's private land is now posted and not available for public recreation.

The Maine tradition of accessing private land for public recreation is coming to an end. In fact, we are beginning to see recreational property leased for private use, something that is common in other states, and this change in the way Mainers traditionally use private land will be another driver of the ongoing effort to buy and conserve the state's most special places.

Some Mainers think the state already owns too much land, and some small, rural communities lose significant tax revenue when private lands are purchased by state and other conservation interests. But so far, the legislature has rejected attempts to significantly limit conservation land purchases.

The major battle continues in Washington County, including Lubec, where without doubt there is a lot of conservation land. Linda and I enjoyed and appreciated some of that conservation land on our recent trip.

Duchesne, Maine's leading birding guide and a Maine legislator, guided our family one morning to a number of great birding spots in Campobello and Lubec. But it was on the South Lubec sandbar, splashing along in our L.L. Bean wellies within sight of the place where my mom grew up, and only a short distance from West Quoddy Head Lighthouse, where my grandfather Ephraim Johnson kept the light for three decades, that Linda and I reached birders' nirvana.

Bob says the sandbar is the best place in Maine to see migrating shorebirds, and he did not exaggerate. The Nature Conservancy purchased the sandbar, and it is now owned by the Department of Inland Fisheries and Wildlife. But the birds rent space there, by the thousands, from early August to mid-September, on their way south.

We spotted, with Bob's help, an amazing array of shorebirds. I wished so much my mother was alive so I could ask her: Did you know what an amazing place this was when you were growing up here? Did you notice all these birds?

We finally made it to Boot Head, another conservation gem purchased and protected by Maine Coast Heritage Trust. It's a 690-acre preserve encompassing spruce/fir forest, peat bogs, rocky coast, and gorgeous pebble beaches. From the cliffs of Boot Head, well, let me just say, it's jaw-droppingly beautiful. And of course, full of birds.

I'm thankful to Maine's conservation community for protecting these special places and making them available to me. And I am especially mindful of what a blessing this will be to my kids, grandkids, and others in the future.

—Central Maine Newspapers (2012)

Changing Maine

Maine has changed a lot in my sixty-two years here, but in many of the ways that count with me, it's changed very little. My heritage is wild and native brook trout and white-tailed deer.

I didn't need today's Hooked-on-Fishing-Not-on-Drugs program offered by Maine's Department of Inland Fisheries and Wildlife. I became addicted to our colorful brook trout at an early age.

Hiking deep into the woods up and over the hill behind our Winthrop home, I'd drop a worm on a small hook into the cold, free-flowing, alder-choked, heavily shaded brook and pull out really nice trout, all of which came home for dinner.

Each summer Mom and Dad would take us way up to Seboomook where my Uncle Johnny and Aunt Flora Mitchell had a camp on the northern end of Moosehead Lake. There we'd troll for and catch lunker landlocked salmon, another important Maine native fish.

In the fall, even though I liked school—especially music and sports—I lived to hunt. How I loved those sunny October Saturday mornings when we'd load our English setter into the car and head for nearby farm fields where Dad's sportsmen's club had stocked pheasants.

I've never forgotten my first pheasant, shot in a cornfield at the end of Maranacook Lake. The dog pointed the bird, the bird flew up out of the corn, and I hit it! Dad was right beside me. I see it still. I'm sure he does too.

Then came those cold November mornings when Dad would get me up well before sunrise to hunt the hills surrounding our town for deer. I rarely saw one and never shot one. And it was the elusiveness, challenge, and camaraderie of deer hunting that made me a lifelong deer hunter.

But oh, how things have changed in Maine. We've lost the deer herd in the North Woods and suffered steeply declining numbers in the rest of the state. There's a home planted right where I shot my first pheasant, and only a couple of southern Maine clubs raise and stock pheasants these days.

Today, my boyhood wild trout brook is a rock-sided gully flowing through a housing development. There are no trout in it. Moosehead Lake's fishery has deteriorated substantially, and the lake now harbors illegally introduced species that eat and compete with the trout and salmon.

I seek my brook trout much farther north at our camp on Sourdnahunk Lake, thankful that civilization has not made it this far to ruin the habitat of Maine's legacy fish. These days I release almost all of the trout I catch. I really don't mind that change.

In fact, this may be the most significant change for me: I love the experiences offered by hunting and fishing, without feeling that I have to kill something every time out. Don't get the wrong idea, however; I still enjoy eating trout and venison.

I have also refocused my fishing attention on smallmouth bass, especially on our rivers, including the Kennebec and Androscoggin. But I also hike into a remote forest to pull one bass after another from an undeveloped jewel of a pond, the pond and surrounding lands now protected and owned by all of us. The experience is not unlike my boyhood fishing adventures in Winthrop.

I recognize that smallies are not native to Maine, but they are what they are, and I like them.

I've also embraced wild turkeys, reintroduced in Maine in 1977 and now prolific. Hunting turkeys is more fun than hunting deer (and I am exceedingly sorry for this blasphemy). The May turkey-hunting season is my new spring obsession.

And most crisp November mornings still find me somewhere on my woodlot, hoping to see that big buck. I've really embraced December's special muzzle-loading season, another new opportunity for Maine hunters.

I've also come to identify with this quote attributed to Scottish writer, John Buchan: "The charm of fishing is that it is the pursuit of what is elusive but attainable—a perpetual series of occasions for hope." You can add hunting to the quote.

Best of all, my ever-hopeful, still-young-at-heart dad still does all of this with me. At eighty-eight years of age, this is a very special privilege—and one thing that hasn't changed.

I don't know if my grandsons will hunt or fish. I've bought each of them a lifetime hunting and fishing license to encourage them in that direction, and they both enjoy fishing with Grampy. We'll see about hunting.

I don't much like change; I do what I can with it. And after six decades, I still like my Maine best.

—My Maine column, *Down East* magazine (July 26, 2011)

Part III:
Family, Friends, and Faith

Teachers Need a Pep Talk

It's time to give teachers a pep talk. Last Thursday I was the luncheon speaker at the retired teachers' annual convention. They wanted to hear about Maine travel, but before I could get to that, it seemed important to let them know they are appreciated.

About every ten years, I write about teachers in this editorial-page column. In 1994 the headline was TEACHERS DON'T HAVE THE SUMMER OFF. In 2001, it was GOOD EDUCATION STILL NEEDS GOOD TEACHERS TEACHING. And in 2010, the headline read TEACHER'S MAIN GOAL AND HOPE IS TO INSPIRE KIDS TO LOVE LEARNING.

In that last column, I wrote that my second-grade teacher, Marie Adell, my high school math teacher Vaughn Curtis, my history teacher Irene Hibbs, my music teacher Frank Stevens, even my basketball coaches, all played important roles in my young life.

One of my business professors at the University of Maine once asked us to write a paper about how the world would be changed by technology in fifty years. I wrote a series of fictional stories set in the future. The professor loved the stories, read them to the class, and told me I should be a writer. I never forgot his encouraging words. And that's what good teachers are: great encouragers.

If you've read any of my previous columns, you know I am married to a first-grade teacher. She says it's good training for dealing with me. Teaching for Linda is a year-round, more-than-full-time profession, and, in her case, obsession. She's always reading, researching, preparing lessons, doing grades, talking with parents, and studying to be the very best teacher she can be.

During the school year, if we are in the living room watching TV, she's cutting out things and working on lesson plans and answering e-mailed messages from parents. When we go on our travel-column trips, I bring a novel; she brings schoolwork.

Two years ago I had to cancel a planned week at camp because she wanted to take a summer course. I just laugh when I hear someone say teachers are lucky because they have summers off. They're definitely not married to one.

While she rarely takes a sick day, if she is seriously sick, she gets up at 5:30 A.M., calls in to alert them to her absence, fires up the computer, and whips up lesson plans for the day, and then drives to school to deliver them. Six years ago a newspaper survey found that the majority of teachers don't use all their sick days. In our school district, four teachers took no sick days. This amazes me, because all you have to do to get sick is spend one December day in an elementary school classroom. Sickness city.

And then they're always changing the textbooks, standards, tests, evaluation procedures, and now, computers. I fear sometimes that we're losing sight of the most important ingredient in our educational system: classroom teachers.

All we can really expect and hope for is that children leave our classrooms having learned to love learning. It is a passion that is critical to their success. I tell students from first grade to college level, if you can read, comprehend what you are reading, and write and speak well, you are going to be a success.

I helped with poetry day last year at the Mount Vernon Elementary School. Three of us who volunteered to help that day were assigned a group of second graders. They read their poems to us, we read poems to them, and then we all worked to create a poem. After forty-five minutes, I was exhausted. I don't know how Linda does it.

This week she is transplanting about two hundred tomato plants—in our living room—for her students to grow and sell to raise money for the local food bank. That's a pretty good lesson right there for the kids, don't you think?

On the morning of my speech the newspaper reported the new grades issued to schools. Mount Vernon Elementary got a grade of C. There was no extra credit awarded for those tomato plants.

I told those retired teachers that instead of grading schools, we should be grading parents. Judging from the applause, I think they agreed. I also told them that teachers work for low wages and little appreciation except from the children, who remember and love them all the rest of their lives. And yes, who give them an A+.

—Central Maine Newspapers (May 8, 2013)

A Sixteenth, a Fiftieth, and a Moose

A sixteenth birthday and a fiftieth wedding anniversary, spanning three generations of the Smith family, brought us all to Camp Phoenix at the edge of Baxter Park for a very special celebration ten days ago.

On the shores of Sourdnahunk Lake gathered brother Gordon with wife Janet and daughters Devon and Erica, sister Edie and sons Nathan and Ezra, our folks Ezra and Ada Smith, and my wife Linda with our kids Rebekah, Joshua, and Hilary.

Throughout the weekend I was constantly reminded of how important our family has been, and remains, in my life. We read a lot about the importance of families, and it is so obviously true that we give it little thought. But when celebrations as momentous as these bring us together, the theories come to life. There is so much strength in a family. We are so much stronger than our individual parts.

Mom and Dad arrived first about midday on Friday and were astonished when Edie and her boys arrived next. My folks didn't realize the entire family was coming all the way to camp to celebrate their fiftieth anniversary. Little Ezra rushed up and spilled the beans. "Nana, everyone's coming!" he exclaimed.

But before the anniversary could be celebrated, Devon's sixteenth birthday cake was lit. Gordon and Janet had driven all the way up with the cake hidden under their seat. As Devon struggled to blow out sixteen candles, we quickly realized that Gordon had mistakenly purchased candles that couldn't be extinguished. At least he claimed it was accidental. We had to drown them in the sink.

Saturday was blustery and cold—October weather—but we hiked and biked and made the most of it. Some read. Some napped. Cards and other games were enjoyed. And we remained on alert for wildlife.

The camp fox was first up, then a doe in the backyard. But no moose, a top priority for young Nathan, who had never seen a moose up close.

The anniversary was celebrated with an evening barbecue. While the wind howled we cooked chicken and burgers on a grill snuggled into our enclosed porch. A massive feast was enjoyed before Edie hauled out a cake for Mom and Dad. This time the candles, with some assistance from the smallest grandchildren, were extinguished with ease.

Then Edie's keyboard appeared, powered by batteries (no electricity, no phone, and no TV in this North Woods paradise), and a number of the more-talented musicians in the family played for us.

When Mom stepped up to the keyboard, the church hymnals came out. We are proud Methodists who sing with gusto. Despite a stiff wind blowing the other way, folks in other camps down below claimed to have heard and enjoyed our hymn sing. Just possibly they were being polite.

Throughout the evening we heard new stories about Mom and Dad's wedding and honeymoon. They were married in Lubec and traveled all the way to East Machias, about twenty miles, only to find that their honeymoon cottage had been rented to someone else. It all worked out and made for a good story. Dad claims the cottages are still there, decrepit and unchanged in fifty years.

Saturday night one of our tents blew down and some of the youngsters ended up sleeping in my Explorer. But the sun was out on Sunday morning. Before everyone left, one task remained.

Nathan had not yet seen his moose. We canceled a second mountain climb and hiked into a bog in back of camp to seek out Mr. Moose. A kingfisher kept us entertained until a meadow hen cruised by and lit in front of us. But time was running out.

Hiding in alders just to the left of a moose trail into the open bog, we first heard a grunt. Then a second grunt a little closer, followed shortly by Hilary whispering, "Something is moving over there."

I tiptoed over with Nathan and we spotted a large moose. Eyes wide, Nate turned to the others, spread his arms, and whispered, "It's huge!"

The large cow moose moseyed into the bog right in front of us and had breakfast. Nate got a close look and seemed especially impressed with the cloud of flies that followed the moose everywhere.

As we wandered the path back to camp, sampling a splendid crop of wild strawberries, mission accomplished, I was supremely satisfied.

A day later, after the fox trotted out her three kits and our doe came out to show us her own family of twin fawns, it seemed like the entire North Woods was participating in our family weekend.

—*Kennebec Journal* (July 28, 1991)

Kids' Accomplishments Ripen in the Spring

May and June are full of hope, a beginning for many, for others the end of a long road. Weddings and graduations dominate the schedule, but sports championships, the arrival of striped bass in the river, garden sprouts and flower blossoms—so much crammed into a few weeks. It leaves me breathless but not wordless.

Let me warn you now: If you don't like bragging about the kids, skip this column.

Endings dominated the month for daughters Rebekah and Hilary. There's a gap of thirteen years between them, but these two are cut from the same mold: talented, focused, confident, independent.

Rebekah's graduation from the University of Maine School of Law came first on May 16, 1998. Third in her class, she was recognized in two awards presented by the alumni and the students as the outstanding member of her class.

As the distinguished ceremony at Portland's magnificent Merrill Auditorium proceeded, and the family passed around the box of tissues, Rebekah snared numerous other awards, but I was so stunned by that time, I can't tell you exactly what they were. All I knew was that I wanted a name tag that read REBEKAH'S DAD.

I presumed when she graduated from Bowdoin that her education had been completed, but what do I know. After working in England and touring Africa, she decided she wanted to be a lawyer.

I don't believe you can have too many lawyers in your family, particularly in my line of work, so I encouraged her to go for it. She'll be clerking for Chief Justice Daniel Wathen of Maine's Supreme Court for a year, and then moving on to the federal level to clerk for Judge Frank Coffin. In case you don't know, let me brag that these are prestigious appointments sought by many and awarded to only a few.

I hope to live long enough to see Rebekah on the US Supreme Court, because she is headed there.

Then there's Hilary. As we sat along the banks of Great Pond at the beautiful home of Fred and Barbara Zinckgraf of Belgrade Lakes for Hilary's piano recital last Saturday, I whispered, "Hil, are you nervous?"

"No," was her succinct reply. Anchoring the lovely afternoon's program of piano and guitar music, played so professionally by the Zinckgrafs' students, Hilary performed flawlessly, then jumped right back into her softball uniform.

We squeezed the recital between playoff softball games. Hil's awesome Maranacook Middle School softball team won morning and afternoon games but fell in the nightcap's championship game to that darned Augusta team (okay, you Hodgkins girls, you are fabulous, I admit it).

During the week the mail brought Hilary's report from the Metropolitan Achievement Tests. If I read it correctly, she scored in the ninety-ninth percentile in the country.

Even though softball and piano are over for a while, Hilary remains focused. And this is truly a girl of heart. When I asked her if she was disappointed not to be able to attend Coach Gary Trafton's excellent soccer camp in July, because we'll be up at our North Woods camp, Hil said, "Oh, no. That's peak fishing, Dad."

Yes, indeed, Hilary, Josh, and I will be out after those wild trout that week, and even Linda is threatening to join us. At least, I purchased Lin's first fishing license and presented it to her on Mother's Day. Hey, cut out the criticism; I got her candy too. (Okay, I did eat most of the candy, but the thought counted . . . I hope.)

Joshua's month has been mostly beginnings. A newfound love for golf has taken him to the Augusta Country Club for lessons from Pete Hatfield, and he's started to beat me on a few holes. Josh has been behind the wheel a lot, practicing for his driver's license test. I await the results with trepidation.

Because he didn't play a spring sport at Maranacook, we got to fish together quite a bit. He can already cast a fly line better than I can, although I keep telling him he's doing it all wrong. And we even got to Fenway once. It's nice having a son for a sidekick, but I'm ever-cognizant that he's already sixteen and will be moving on soon.

On the honor roll, Josh seems to have set his sights on becoming a lawyer too. What is this? Something in our water? I'm trying to steer him toward a career as a fishing guide, but having little luck so far.

And oh yes, tomorrow marks the nineteenth year since Linda and I took our wedding vows. (Don't worry; I'll pick some flowers for her from the back field.)

There may be beginnings and endings this month, but some things never change, do they?

—*Kennebec Journal* (June 16, 1998)

A Lifelong Romance with Retail

Our shopping future may be in the wide aisles of Wal-Mart, but our past was in the narrow, cluttered aisles of local five-and-dimes.

When Alfred Senter announced last week that Senter's Department Store in Brunswick will close after eighty-three years of providing Maine people with outstanding service, melancholy settled over me, swept in by my own memories of Wilson's Dollar Stores and buffeted by other names like Unobsky's and Treworgy's.

The local five-and-dime is dead, buried by the automobile and discount mart. We'll drive to the new Augusta mall, passing empty stores in our own towns, cursing the lack of service and the congestion at the mall, forgetting our role in the murder of Senter's, Wilson's, and other community retail stores.

I had a romance with retail from a very early age when I started out in the business by counting inventory at Wilson's, where my dad worked his way up from clerk to part owner. Wilson's was a five-and-dime with everything from shoes to hardware, candy, toys, and more. Wilson's grew from a single store in Winthrop, founded by my namesake, George "Squanto" Wilson, into a chain of stores from Lincoln to Norway, including Auburn, Hallowell, Gardiner, and Livermore Falls.

I worked in all the stores at one time or another. It was an incredible education in what is now a bygone era.

The urban renewal project that left a hole where Wilson's once stood on Winthrop's Main Street left an even bigger hole in my heart. The bulldozers and building movers removed my boyhood home, where I cooked peanuts, sorted work pants, stacked sneakers, swept floors, and checked out customers.

Oh, the smell of those hot roasted cashews drove this growing youngster crazy! I'm sure I ate up all the profit on those. But it is the customers I remember best.

This was the era when service was more than a slogan. We waited on customers, served them with a smile, and thanked them profusely when they made a purchase. The customer was always right. A lot of visiting went on at the cash register, and I developed a knack for ringing up sales while talking about last night's basketball game.

I learned a lot about serving customers from Dad, who often rose from bed on Christmas Eve to respond to a frantic call from a father who had neglected to purchase gifts for his kids. Dad would trudge down to the store, open up, and wait on his customer. He never said it, but I always knew that he really did it for the kids.

People flocked to Wilson's in Winthrop from Readfield, Mount Vernon, Wayne, Monmouth, and the far reaches of Kennebec County. I met people from every state in the Union during the summer months, including some rather famous folks, like pro golfer Bob Rosburg.

I am still known hereabouts as Ezra Smith's kid, by all those customers who knew Dad in the store and appreciated his cheery service.

As I got older, my store assignments grew in responsibility, but I never liked working in the warehouse, delivering goods in the truck, or laboring in other positions that took me away from the retail stores. That connection to the customer was the thing I enjoyed the most.

I think about that today whenever I am in line at a big-box check out. It is all so impersonal. The clerk doesn't know me. The programmed response, "Thank you for shopping at _____" just isn't the same.

In these stores, I can't find someone to wait on me to save my soul. The peanuts are locked up in cans, and the only smell is that of disinfectant.

Everyone's in a hurry, there's no laughing, no fun. I don't think it's much fun to work in retail stores today. At least, the employees don't look to me like they're having the kind of fun I always had at Wilson's.

Mr. Senter lasted longer than most, and I'm sure he is suffering now. But he can be proud of his store's long record and tradition of customer service.

I don't know if Maine will have any small retail department stores left at the turn of the twenty-first century. But I did notice that next to Senter's letter, announcing the store's closure in the *Kennebec Journal*, was an ad for Renys. Bob Reny fights on, nearly alone now. Go get 'em, Bob!

—*Kennebec Journal* (July 6, 1992)

Reflections on Fatherhood

Yesterday fathers throughout Maine were applauded. We received funny greeting cards, were showered with gifts, and generally encouraged to do whatever we wanted that day. I'm sure some played golf, others fished. Some probably spent the day in the hammock, canoeing a local stream, or camping in a favorite spot.

For me, Father's Day goes both ways, featuring an opportunity to honor my dad and my father-in-law, whom we are lucky to have, and my own celebrations organized by my kids. A look back, if you will, as well as a look ahead. The day gave me a chance to think about fatherhood, to reminisce about the good times, to regret the missed opportunities, and to evaluate my performance as a dad.

Fatherhood is attending the piano recital of Josh and Hilary two weeks ago, flushed with pride at their virtuosity. It also included taking turns at running them over to Belgrade every Tuesday for lessons, and applauding every time they practiced.

There is a good dose of volunteering that comes with this fatherhood role. This year for me it's major league softball. The Seminoles lost every game, but we achieved our goals: to have fun and to improve with every game.

Without doubt we're the most improved team in the league, and I have been fortunate that other dads, including Stan Eller, Dave Riggs, and John Tyler, have been there constantly to help. It has also been a pleasure to have the coaching assistance of thirteen-year-old Josh. Most of the girls will listen to him (except for his sister!). Oh yes, mothers have helped a great deal, too, but this column is about fathers.

Fatherhood is taking the kids hiking deep in Baxter Park for an overnight at Little Wassataquoik lean-to. I insisted that we could get by with blankets rather than sleeping bags for this August trip, and oh, I was so wrong. We just about froze to death.

Fatherhood involves making mistakes, too, and displaying our ignorance. My kids learned early on that Father does not always know best (that role is reserved for mothers), or even know what he's talking about a lot of the time.

Fatherhood is insisting that chores be done. We also serve as enforcers of household rules, values, and laws. I raise my voice on occasion, but I think the kids know that they can get away with a lot. I'm a pushover. But hey, these kids are lovable.

Fatherhood is about love, too, although many of us don't mention it. It must be in a look, a caress, an offer to take them to Boston for a Red Sox game. Fathers display love, but in obscure ways.

A lot of this is setting a good example. Few of us are going to qualify for sainthood, but it is important to establish some values and performance standards for our kids. Sometimes this simply means buckling a seat belt, or giving up smoking. Language is important, and I often bite my tongue and swallow those cusswords when the kids are around. I'd be as embarrassed as you-know-what to hear my kids swear in public, because I'd know that you'd know they learned those words at home.

So fatherhood also involves changing one's habits to set a good example for the kids. I clearly remember my dad giving up beer while we kids were growing up. (Sorry, Dad; that one didn't take!)

Fatherhood is getting one's hands dirty with the kids, planting a garden together, digging for worms, painting the house. We insist on chores, and I took real delight when Josh became old enough to ride the lawn mower. I hate to mow the lawn! Okay, now you've found us out. Fatherhood is about getting the kids to do our chores.

As the years progress, the father's job changes. As Rebekah marched off to Bowdoin College, my job seemed to involve a lot of paperwork, loans, moving and heavy lifting, and telephone calls.

When she moved to England, it was care packages from home and longer-distance phone calls, with a hefty dose of worrying. When she took off for a six-week tour of Africa, the worrying increased, especially after we received a postcard saying she'd enjoying skydiving!

I do so much writing and calling in my work that I'm not very good at it with the kids. Rebekah gets after me quite often. Now that she's on her way back to Maine to attend law school, I suppose I'm going to be traveling to the big city more often to see her. I'll be taking this fatherhood job on the road. And I guess that's a never-ending road, too.

It is a father's lot to watch the kids grow up too fast and to spend the balance of our lives trying to catch up with them, wherever they land when they jump out of the nest (or an airplane).

Fatherhood is time, and we never have enough of it.

—*Kennebec Journal* (June 19, 1995)

When It's Time to Say Good-bye

You think about a lot of things when your mother is dying in the hospital.

You think about how precious life is. Long ago, Mom and Dad taught each of their children how to live. But when we received the awful news in April that Mom's lung cancer had spread to her bones, and when it became clear she would not be leaving the hospital, life never seemed so precious.

You think about her life, her impact on you, her influence on so many others through her school and church work. And you tell her all that while you reminisce.

There was a lot of laughter in those final days, amidst the tears.

You think that few people can be so selfless, so devoted to others, to their families, and to God, as she was. You wish you could be. You think about that a lot in those last days. You reorder your priorities and make lots of resolutions.

You think about the column you wrote for her a few years ago on Mother's Day, in which you wondered what you would have done without her. And now you wonder what you will do. You think about death.

In her final days, Mom taught me how to die. Her faith sustained her, and she greeted death with a smile. She knew where she was going, and it is a joyous place. She tested our faith to be sure we would see her in Heaven.

You think about medical care, especially terminal care. Dr. Jim Brassard's career was fulfilled—even if he never treats another patient—with his extraordinary care of my mother. He gave us the gift of four final days with Mom, in which she

164

was comfortable and able to communicate with us from time
to time.

When Dr. Brassard took time from his busy day to travel
to Winthrop to pay his respects during visiting hours at the
funeral home, we knew that Mom had touched him too. Like-
wise for Dr. McKee, Mom's skilled surgeon, who attended her
funeral.

You think about the wonderful nurses who attended Mom
and the rest of us as we moved into the hospital for those last
four days and crowded her room, the hallway, and the family
visitors' room Their compassion and care were extraordinary.

You think about all who brought food, fellowship, music,
and prayers to the hospital and, later, to our homes, and you
are grateful.

You think about your own friends and associates. I had to
leave my lobbyist's post at the legislature while Mom was in
the hospital those final four days, and legislators could not
have been more kind and considerate. Flowers and cards and
calls from them and many others throughout the state sustained me. There is no partisanship, no advantage taken, when
tragedy strikes. The hugs of those who were on the opposite
side of me on some key issues were just as sincere and strong
as those from my allies.

You think about your siblings. Brother Gordon guided Mom
through the medical world over the final six months of her
illness, and sister Edie took over to organize her funeral and
write her obituary. I know Mom was very proud of Gordon
and Edie.

You think about your dad, losing his partner of fifty-two
years, and you hug him more than you ever have in your life.

You think about funerals, cemeteries—so many details at a time when your grief is so great. The professionals at Roberts Funeral Home were extraordinary. Lyn Roberts Reed even cooked a meal for our family. I guess that's not an official part of their services.

You pore through old albums, selecting photos to display at the visiting hours and reception. That was such a joyful experience. I urge everyone to take lots of photos of your families.

You think about West Quoddy Head Lighthouse in Lubec, where Mom's grandfather, Ephraim Johnson, kept the light for twenty-six years, and you know that her light now shines brightly in Heaven.

Five hundred people paid their respects during visiting hours, and even more attended Mom's spectacular funeral, where we all enjoyed a rousing hymn sing, as she had specified. Reverend Cathy Anderson read the eulogy I wrote for Mom, the most difficult writing assignment I ever had, and she did it beautifully.

You wake up the day after it is all over, the funeral completed, the cemetery lot selected, the house still filled with food and flowers, and you are drained of energy. You walk around in a daze, unfocused, cut loose finally—reluctantly— fifty-one years later, from the umbilical cord.

If you are blessed with a living mom, give her a hug for me this Mother's Day. And then give her another hug for you.

—*Kennebec Journal* (May 10, 2000)

The Sun Rises—and Sets—on Lubec

Lubec was a thriving town when my mother was born there, even though it was the end of the Earth. The highway ended in Lubec. You had to take a ferry to travel farther.

Water Street was packed with businesses, but it was the oceanfront fish-packing plants that dominated the town and provided many of the jobs. Grandmother Searles packed sardines, and my Canadian-born grandfather was a fish inspector.

On a summer visit, I can remember laughing when I first spotted the gas station name "Irving" on the nearby Canadian island of Campobello. What a funny name for a gas station, I thought. Little did I know!

There were plenty of jobs then. My uncle Mervelle Searles worked at American Can, providing millions of cans for all those sardines.

David Jones was my mother's father's brother's daughter's son, a second cousin to me, but a young man we always called Cousin David. He began working for the state park service right out of high school, and eventually became caretaker at West Quoddy Head Lighthouse, perhaps Maine's most scenic state park.

David's work at West Quoddy continued the sense of ownership my family has always enjoyed there since my great-grandfather kept the light burning for three decades. Lubec began to die when the herring vanished and the packing plants followed.

When American Can moved on, my uncle moved with the company, taking a job in New Jersey. The Peacock family struggled to maintain Lubec's ties to the sea, even packing urchins for the Japanese market. New jobs materialized when Atlantic salmon aquaculture facilities were built just offshore.

But Water Street slowly died, filled with boarded-up buildings, dilapidated fish plants, and rotting docks. A large bridge linking Lubec and Campobello helped to move tourists through the area, but few stopped in Lubec for more than gas and groceries.

David Jones thrived out at West Quoddy Head Light. He was a sweet kid who greeted every visitor with a "Hi, how you doing?" He was personally embarrassed if even a single blade of grass was uncut at the park. David attracted new friends all day, every day, and was highly regarded throughout the park service. He was devoted to his mother, and continued to live at home after both his father and his stepfather died.

David always exclaimed what a thrill it was every morning to crest the hill and see that red-striped lighthouse sitting on the bluff over the ocean on the easternmost point in the United States.

I remember his visit when he came to Augusta to receive special recognition for twenty-five years of work for the park service. He was so proud. He met Governor Angus King and had his photo taken with him. It was a very meaningful ceremony for David.

Recent visits to Lubec have shown a town struggling to survive. Some spruced-up historic homes are now bed-and-breakfasts. Residents cobble together a living picking blueberries, packing sardines in the last remaining plant, growing Atlantic salmon, making Christmas wreaths, digging bloodworms and clams.

It's not an easy life amidst the splendid scenery. You can't eat scenery, as they say.

On Thursday, July 19, 1992, Stinson Seafood, owned by Connors Bros. Ltd. of Canada, announced that its Lubec sardine plant was closing. One hundred jobs were lost. The closure was historic. Lubec by the sea will no longer can sardines. My grandmother wouldn't have believed it possible.

Options for those who lost their jobs are limited. "It wouldn't be such a blow for us if there were other options on the horizon," noted town manager Nancy Mathews.

Four days prior to the announcement, forty-eight-year-old David Jones got out of bed and fell to the floor, dead of a heart attack. His funeral brought out the town, with residents and friends filling every pew in the church and standing all around the sanctuary. Three pews were filled with David's coworkers from the park service.

In his casket, David looked so serene and dignified in his park uniform. Atop the casket was a photo of David receiving the award for twenty-five years of service from Governor King and Conservation Commissioner Ron Lovaglio.

My sister Edie delivered a eulogy that captured the essence of our cousin David so well—a loving, caring, friendly, responsible young man of whom we were so proud. West Quoddy will never have another like him.

There is talk of dedicating a park bench to David. If they do, the grass around it better be well trimmed and up to his meticulous standards.

A sense of sadness hung over us as we left the church in Lubec where my folks were married. My mom died last year.

David died this year. Lubec has been dying for more than two decades.

It doesn't seem right in a place that is so beautiful.

—*Kennebec Journal* (1992)

Update: I've written this Lubec lament several times over the years. A few years ago the local high school closed. The medical center is now the biggest employer. Summer tourism is flourishing, but the winters are long, the jobs few, the prospects no better than when I wrote this first column in 1992.

The Gardening Obsession

The large cucumber is held up rather tentatively for Dad's approval at my vegetable stand in front of Wilson's Dollar Stores on Winthrop's Maine Street. Dad worked there. The photo, now fifty-five years old, sits on my bookshelf.

I was ten years old and quite an entrepreneur, using a 4-H vegetable garden to rustle up cash. Two signs are on the table: CUCUMBERS, 2 FOR 5 CENTS. TOMATOES, 3 FOR 10 CENTS. Those tomatoes look especially tasty.

Not being one who gets rid of anything, the TOMATOES sign sits next to the photo on my bookshelf, a wonderful reminder of a blissful childhood.

I didn't get rich in the garden, but it was honest work, especially for a kid. I also sold green beans door to door, riding my bike all over town. Thank God I didn't turn out to be a farmer. It's just a recipe for going broke these days.

But fifty-five years later, I am still gardening, albeit as a helper for my obsessive gardening wife. Burned out by a childhood of gardening, I'd gotten away from it until Linda and I moved to Mount Vernon and inherited garden space behind the house. We actually planted our first garden before officially owning the house, on a miserably hot Memorial Day weekend when the air was choked with blackflies. Vivid memories, still.

Previous owners had planted a wonderful asparagus bed out back and an amazing stand of raspberries along the driveway. The asparagus bed wore out and a moose destroyed the raspberry bushes one year; they are still producing, although not

171

as prolifically as they did during our banner years, when we'd harvest as many as a hundred quarts of luscious berries.

Gardening is fraught with anxiety, where your most diligent care can be defeated by weather, wild critters, blight, disease, insects, and even the family pets. We had a dog who loved to eat the raspberries. He'd pluck them right off the stems. One year the dog rolled in the green beans and killed them. Discouragement may set in when the anticipated first tasty shoots of broccoli are gobbled up in the night by deer.

The romance of growing one's own food may evaporate with the first sighting of the massive and ugly tomato hornworm. It would give anyone the heebie-jeebies.

One year, angry that some critter was knocking over our corn to feast on the cobs, I rigged up a shotgun with a flashlight on top and snuck out one night to find a fat skunk waddling down the corn row. I dispatched him and ran for cover. It was a couple of days before I could stand to get near enough to remove him from the garden. We stopped growing corn.

I also shoot all the woodchucks. Those buggers eat everything, including violets.

After trying every remedy to discourage deer, we settled on an electric fence. It's done remarkably well. But one day, Lin looked out the kitchen window to see a bunch of turkeys flopping up and over the fence to chow down. Oh, if only I could have videotaped her, running across the lawn, waving her arms and screeching at those very surprised turkeys. They never returned.

Some years, with a great deal of perseverance and luck, you get something to eat after the wild animals are through. And somewhere along the gardening trail, I began, again, to enjoy it, although not as much as Linda.

Last year she got a 14-by-28-foot hoop house, a huge, plastic-wrapped structure that produces vegetables year-round. Fresh greens in the winter are amazing. And this year, her tomato plants reached all the way to the ceiling!

E. B. White wrote about a gardening book that its publisher claimed was "welcomed by an increasing number of American people who, fed up with the pressure of city living, are going back to the land for their livelihood."

White wrote, "That shows that publishers do not understand the situation. Pressure of city living? No pressure which I ever knew in town compares with the pressure of country living. Never before in my life have I been so pressed as the last two years. Forty acres can push a man hard even when he isn't in debt. Pressure! I've been on the trot now for a long time, and don't know whether I'll ever get slowed down."

'Tis true. Country living is pressure-filled. And I'm not just talking about gardens. I am rushing to get the wood into the basement for the coming winter while splitting next year's supply and storing it in the woodshed. I am way behind on the brush cutting. I swear if I stopped doing it, in five years Linda and I would be living in the deep woods.

My summer to-do list still contains too many things to do, including some key painting projects. Heck, I haven't even gotten out fishing as much as I wanted to. And the fall hunting seasons approach. Time to put up the tree stands and do some scouting for deer.

Wait a minute; maybe if I remove that electric fence around the garden, I won't have to look for deer. They'll come to me!

173

High School Reunion

A fortieth high school reunion can be an unpleasant look in the mirror, wondering who that gray-haired old buzzard is staring back at you. Mine was a very pleasant surprise. Apprehension was quickly set aside by the real pleasure of seeing friends who had dropped out of my life so many years ago.

The Augusta Country Club put out a delicious buffet as a few dozen survivors of the Winthrop High School class of 1966 gathered with spouses to find out how our lives had turned out. Actually, the good news is that most members of our class of 107 are still alive and kicking. Well, maybe not kicking; shuffling might be more accurate.

Alas, I can't say the same for our high school. The old building is gone. So are most of the businesses on Main Street. Who could have imagined the end of McNamara's Restaurant? Bruneau's Market? Wilson's Dollar Stores?

We are reminded that so much of life is transitory and fleeting. I'm old enough to remember the bowling alley at Maranacook Lodge, where a kid set up the pins after you knocked them down. I remember trains delivering passengers at the railroad depot at the end of my street.

I remember Memorial Drive when it was only a handful of camps. It's now crowded with expensive year-round homes, Maine's story written in a once-small town. And of course, I remember a bunch of young kids full of vim and vigor. Ah, but we've aged well.

Wife Linda had prepared me for the event, warning that many of my classmates are probably retired. I doubted it. She was right.

Mel Wade has retired from the military and a second career as well. Barry Scott retired three years ago from teaching high school math. Others have retired but still work part-time, including Jeff Bond, retired from the National Guard but now working part-time for them as a civilian, and Greg Foster, down to two days a week at his law firm.

When I groused to these guys that I was still working full-time, they said, "Hey, all you do is hunt and fish!" Well, of course; that's my work.

I was fascinated by some of the choices my classmates had made in their lives. Lew Caraganis, the smartest guy in a class of smart kids, went to Bowdoin College, kicked around for a while, built boats, sailed the seas, and anchored in North Carolina, where he has his own construction company. He described his odyssey to find something significant to do with his life—a search that certainly resonated with many of us.

Mark Stevens went even further, to the far reaches of the wilderness of British Columbia, where he carved out a home, raised a family, and found satisfying work. His kids are scattered all over the place now. One is a professional beach volleyball player.

Of course, many shared news of their kids, and quite a few could trot out stories about grandchildren, so I got in a few licks bragging about my own grandson Addison.

As we went around the room, each classmate speaking about his or her life, work, and family, I was carried back to the old brick building where we had spent four long years—without a clue, really. Oh, if I could only go back, knowing what I know now.

Well, some would argue that I know less today than I did in 1966, and in some ways, that's true. At age fifty-seven, I guess I'm on the downward slope of life, shedding brain cells as I shush down the trail. At least I wasn't the only one with a spare part. The stent that cleared my clogged artery was topped by a new kidney received recently by the still-youthful Martha Ashley Kelly.

We shared our concerns for a fellow classmate struggling with cancer, and signed a card for him, a reminder of the fact that good health is a special blessing, never taken for granted.

While many of the—well, they're still girls to me—looked marvelous, us guys looked like a bunch of guys in their fifties. What's that you say? We *are* a bunch of guys in our fifties? Okay, but you don't have to be so smug about it.

I remember when the age of twenty seemed old, and I thought anyone over fifty was ancient. Now I've joined those ranks. Oh, well; this reunion was a night of memories, updated. I can't wait for the next one.

—Central Maine Newspapers (September 20, 2006)

Letting Go of Josh

Letting go of a treasure is always difficult, especially one that you've loved, nurtured, polished, protected, and admired from near and far for twenty-two years. All the way to the Manchester airport last Thursday, transporting son Josh, who graduated from college last May, to a plane that would take him to his new job in Oregon, I pondered: Did I teach him everything he needs to know? Were there any last-minute instructions that I had failed to mention? Can I let him go?

The closer we got to Manchester, the more I panicked. Of course, there is more he needs to know! Of course, I have fallen short in his education! But of course, he is ready to step out into the real world as a young adult.

For Pete's sake, he's traveled all the way around the world, backpacked through the jungles of Thailand, visited Mother Theresa's orphanage in India, stood on the Great Wall of China, communed with refugees in Tanzania, and even sat through a four-hour speech in Cuba by Fidel Castro. At the tender age of twenty-two, Josh has already visited more countries than me, and in many ways, is much worldlier.

Sadly, all of this education has made him a person with liberal tendencies—a Democrat, if I must confess all here—perhaps my biggest failing as a Republican parent. Nevertheless, I am immensely proud of Josh. He's an independent thinker, a young man of great empathy for the poor and marginalized citizens of the world, who puts his words and deeds where his heart is.

He has chosen to give a year of public service, and that, too, makes me proud. He'll be working for Holy Cross Associated, serving in a program for the homeless in Portland, Oregon, and living modestly for the next twelve months. I know not where he'll go from there. Sometimes that scares me.

Everything he found necessary to possess for the next year went into two packs on Thursday—less stuff than I take on a week's fishing trip. He's a well-organized young man, and that is not a trait he got from his dad.

As we drove from Mount Vernon to Manchester, scenes passed by that were not visible out the car window. Josh, on the front porch with his tiny backpack and casting rod, with the toothless grin of a five-year-old, ready for our spring fishing expedition to Maranacook Lake for white perch. It's one of my all-time favorite photos.

Josh with his first large trout from Sourdnahunk Lake, where he learned to fly-fish, creating his own unique casting motion by ignoring my efforts to teach him to cast. I gave up when it became apparent that he was casting better and farther than I was. Josh with a six-pound brook trout during our amazing trip to Labrador's Little Minipi Lodge the summer before his senior year in high school.

Josh, last weekend, with a huge smallmouth bass taken during a leisurely canoe trip down the Androscoggin River from Dixfield to Canton.

Hey, all those images are of Josh and fish! Go figure.

Of course, there are many other images and memories: graduations, ball games, home, camp, church, school, and family activities. But it's our shared love of fishing, I think, that most closely binds us as father and son.

And that was my strategy all along: imprint Maine's wondrous waters and fighting fish, those outdoor experiences that make life in Maine "the way it should be," hoping he'll return to his home waters when he is finished wandering and experiencing the world.

There must be more than woods and waters here for him, I understand that, and as much as any Maine resident, I will be hounding the governor and legislature and business leaders to create an economy and opportunities that will bring Josh home.

During a competitive family card game the other night, I proclaimed our work on Josh to be completed. "Job done," I shouted. "You're on your own now."

Everyone laughed, because they knew I didn't mean it. Even as I pulled away from the curb at the Manchester airport, eyeing Josh for a final time as he stood in line, waiting to check his bags with the skycap, another scrap of information popped into my head. I pulled over and rolled down the passenger window.

"Josh, don't forget to get name and address tags from the skycap and put them on your bags," I said.

"Sure, Dad; I know." Of course he does.

And with that big smile I miss so much already, he leaned down to the open window and said simply, "Bye, Dad."

"Good-bye, Josh," said my voice, while my heart said, "Come home soon."

—*Kennebec Journal* (August 4, 2004)

Update: Josh now works for My Brother's Keeper, an outstanding, privately funded program that serves the poor in the Brockton, Massachusetts, area. He and his wife Kelly would love to relocate to Maine, but haven't been able to find the jobs they'd need to make that move. I'm still wishing. Still hoping.

Church Shopping

A friend is church shopping, a phenomenon I assume is like restaurant shopping. This friend suggested that newspapers could help church shoppers by publishing church reviews similar to reviews of restaurants and movies. Given that Linda and I write a weekly travel column for these newspapers, I immediately saw a new writing opportunity: "The Travelin' Maine(rs) go to church!"

This column would help church shoppers by presenting only the very best church experiences, so they could avoid any unpleasant visits, and find the church that most closely matches their expectations. In this ecumenical spirit, hopefully falling short of blasphemy, we begin our review of area churches today.

On our Sunday-morning visits to area churches, we will rate the following: parking capacity, outside and inside appearance, comfort of pews, music (divided into categories of youth choir, adult choir, and organist), minister's appearance, sermons (quality and length), church school, nursery, outside missions, budget, and congregation.

Once all the items are scored, one to five stars will be awarded—one star representing churches to be avoided, and five stars indicating even the most cynical attendee could be happy here.

Our first visit was to the North New England Community Church, where Pastor Joseph Weldon ekes out a modest living ministering to the souls of a small but growing congregation. Pastor Weldon is a large man dressed in a dark blue polyester

suit (-5 points) set off by a bright yellow tie (-2), matching the
sunny day which greeted us (+5) as we parked in the ample
paved parking lot very handy to the front door (+10).

The church is the traditional white clapboard building
favored by countrified yuppies, with a belfry and bell (+100).
The hard wooden pews without cushions (-25) offered little
comfort, and the sanctuary was dark with little decoration
except for a mural at the front (-15).

Our spirits were lifted, however, when the adult choir
marched in, led by a spunky piano player and singing a jazzy
rendition of "When the Saints Come Marching In" (+50). The
choir lacked robes (-15), but was well balanced, with very fine
voices.

As the service began, the congregation sang with gusto
(+10) a favorite hymn (+10 for avoiding unfamiliar hymns).
The organist did a fine job (+20). Then the congregation
remained standing to greet one another (+5). We received a
very warm welcome, and were pleased to see that the children were well dressed and reasonably well behaved (+25).
Although sprinkled with old people, there appeared to be a
good mix of younger families (+50).

The service moved quickly, but there was no youth choir
(-15). We noted that a nursery was available downstairs (+15).
In mid-service children left to attend Sunday school, which is
always held during the service, allowing parents to fulfill their
church obligation in just one hour each week (+250).

Pastor Weldon read the Scriptures well, and we enjoyed
his friendly, uplifting voice (+5). However, his sermon was
a disappointment. On this Sunday he seemed melancholy.
His message—that we are all headed to Hell in a handbasket

unless we repent of our sinful ways—was not what we hoped to hear. We were expecting a pleasing message that did not challenge us. Pastor Weldon preached for nearly twenty minutes, exceeding by ten minutes the ideal length for a sermon (-30 for message and -40 for length).

The service lasted sixteen minutes over the expected one hour (-50). However, the coffee fellowship time that followed added greatly to our experience, with superior coffee (+20) and exceptional pastries (+30). Those partaking were by and large people like us (+100), who took time to visit and inquire about us (+30). We felt very comfortable.

We asked about their church missions and discovered they support all the politically correct organizations. No money appeared to be going to conservative religious nuts or organizations (+50). Their overall church budget of $130,000 is modest, indicating that we would not be required to turn over much of our own income should we decide to join (+200).

Overall, the North New England Community Church scored 788 points, giving it three stars. With improvement from Pastor Weldon (better clothes, shorter and more-pleasing sermons), cushions for the pews, and a youth choir, this church would aspire to four or perhaps even five stars in the future.

Your membership might make the difference. Check it out next Sunday!

Update: This was written for my editorial-page column last year, but my editor refused to publish it, afraid readers would think I was serious. WARNING: This is satire. Sort of.

N'wawlins

Twenty minutes from our N'wawlins ("New Orleans," for the linguistically challenged) hotel, a "Swamp Tour" offers alligators, snakes, and more. Only this sinfully delicious (and maybe deliciously sinful) city could make a tour out of a swamp.

Some might say the French Quarter is the real N'wawlins swamp, where naked dancing and worse (some would say better) is featured on the infamous (some would say famous) and dingy Bourbon Street, street musicians aggressively seek your attention and money, and wandering the narrow, historical (some would say hysterical) byways with a large container of one's favorite alcoholic beverage is not only legal but encouraged. Indeed, you feel naked *without* a drink in your hand.

N'wawlins is not for the prudish. A certain liberal enlightenment was necessary for the native conservative. I walked around with a perpetual grin on my face. So this is what Sodom and Gomorrah is like!

Frankly, I've never seen anything quite like N'wawlins— which made our visit there last week all the more fascinating. This bayou city is a feast for the palate, ears, and eyes, featuring colorful and intricate 250-year-old buildings, and stunning ferns and flowers draped above, on, and below black, wrought-iron balconies that hang over every French Quarter street.

We weren't there for Mardi Gras, but strange people in bizarre costumes paraded by us all day long. I think they were the natives.

We shopped for books in William Faulkner's old home; guzzled ice-cold beer in the cool, dark bar called Napoleon's

(remodeled in the nineteenth century to serve as emperor
Bonaparte's exile following his defeat at Waterloo), next door
to the place where Andrew Jackson plotted the definitive battle
that led the British to surrender to Jackson and America's desire
for independence; stood before the oldest Catholic cathedral
in America, where Pope Paul once stood, and were startled
when the cathedral's bells suddenly tolled to announce the
election of a new Pope; and tapped our feet to jazz in a bar
where Louis Armstrong and other jazz legends once played.

Imagine a bar where Robert E. Lee, the Marquis de Lafay-
ette, Alexis Grand Duke of all the Russias, Oscar Wilde,
Buffalo Bill Cody, Enrico Caruso, Sarah Bernhardt, John L.
Sullivan, Babe Ruth, and P. T. Barnum all enjoyed a beverage!

Well, you don't have to imagine the food here. Crawfish
creole, Cajun-blackened steak, shrimp gumbo, jambalaya,
étouffée, and the most amazing sandwiches: po'boys stuffed
with ham and roast beef from Mother's, dripping with the
leavings of gravy and bits of roast beef after the roasting is
done—it's a two-dozen-napkins delight; a muffuletta from
Central Grocery (where they were invented), a huge rounded
Italian bread covering a mountain of Italian meats and cheeses,
topped with an unbelievably tasty olive salad mix—so good
we purchased a quart of the mix to bring home—muffulettas
in Mount Vernon!

There is no greater breakfast experience in the world of
food than to bite into a hot beignet (a donut without the hole,
but this doesn't begin to describe it) while the massive amount
of powdered sugar on top puffs into the air and covers your
shirt and pants—ha, ha, ha, says I, this is why I'm wearing
white today!

We splurged for dinner at Commander's Palace in the Garden District—often mentioned as one of the world's finest restaurants, where famous chefs like Emeril Lagasse and Paul Prudhomme once reigned—and enjoyed a world-class dining experience of superb service and sumptuous food in an exquisite environment, topped by Bananas Foster—a flaming performance dessert also original to N'wawlins.

Walking the historic streets, you are invited to sit for performances by street musicians of jazz, blues, or Cajun music. The soaring sounds of Doreen the Clarinet Queen brought us back to the steps of the Louisiana Supreme Court many times, where we soaked up the sun and the sounds of Doreen and her band.

The ragtag brass band of Jackson Square provided hours of splendid, foot-stomping jazz each day. The band included a slightly different cast of talented performers daily, and they appeared to be enjoying their beverages and music as much as the tourists who gathered around the square to listen. The fellow with the tuba of a thousand dents held together with duct tape was our favorite, but the elderly gent who glided around the square, dancing with a broom, was pretty special too.

A night of dining and dancing to Cajun music at Mulate's, and a more sedate evening of jazz (and, of course, more dining) at Palm Court Jazz Cafe were also special.

The week sped by as we floated through the French Quarter on the sights, sounds, and scents that define N'wawlins. Today reality sets in, and I await a spring that seems as distant as my new favorite city down on the Mississippi bayou.

Beat your feet to N'wawlins someday.

—Central Maine Newspapers (April 27, 2005)

Graduation Day Regrets

I'm sorry that my last child, Hilary, graduated last Sunday from Maranacook High School. Lin and I are getting a bird's-eye view of the empty nest. No wonder those birds fly south for the winter instead of sitting in that cold, empty nest, missing their youngsters.

There is so much to be sorry for now.

I'm sorry I didn't attend every single one of Hilary's school and extracurricular events. Oh, I attended most. But now—now that they're over . . . now that there will never be another one . . . not a single one—I realize how special they are (were). I can't go back and attend those that I missed.

I'm sorry I didn't pay more attention to Hilary's writing. I was astonished last week by the clarity and beauty of her poems in a new edition of the school's publication, *Tingley Brook*. How did she learn to write that well? Where did those words come from?

I'm sorry I didn't say thank-you more often to Hil's teachers. She had some exceptional teachers, from Mount Vernon Elementary School all the way through Maranacook. One of them, Lois Beedy, retired last week, and I got to thank her in person, but I'm sorry I didn't send every one of Hilary's special teachers handwritten thank-you notes each year.

I'm sorry I didn't turn Hilary on to hunting. She has her own mind, and it never once led her into the woods to shoot something. Some of you are now applauding, I know. But I'm sorry, nonetheless.

I'm sorry I didn't teach Hilary more of the life skills she'll need now—how to change the oil in her car, how to identify different screwdrivers, how to balance a checkbook. She probably knows some of these things, but I didn't teach her about them. Of course, I don't know some of this stuff either!

I'm sorry for all the times I ordered her to clean her room or pick up the house. It did no good, and it always caused an angry exchange.

I'm sorry I didn't listen more carefully to what she was telling me. I'm sorry I was so demanding. Of course you want to establish high expectations for your children and demand the highest level of performance, but I was rather unforgiving of anything less than perfection. She will tell you this is an understatement.

I remember once when Hil brought home a report card featuring an A+, three A's, and an A-. I'm sorry I inquired what went wrong in the class with the A-.

I'm sorry I ever doubted that she was getting her work done on time. As far as I can tell, she did a superb job (third in her class), although too often (by my standards) getting her work done at the last possible minute. It sometimes made me frantic—and irritated.

Have you ever arisen at three A.M. to find your child doing her homework? She seems most proud of the distinction as her class's greatest female procrastinator. I'm sorry I didn't understand how that could work for her.

I'm sorry we didn't do more kayaking together, hike more of Baxter's magnificent mountains together, cast flies to more of Sourdnahunk's eager trout together. Yes, we did quite a bit of that—but I wish we'd done more.

187

I'm sorry I didn't take Hilary on a special trip—like the trip son Josh and I took to fish in Labrador before he graduated from high school. Perhaps it's not too late. We'll talk about it (and it need not be a fishing trip!).

Last week, prior to the family graduation party, Linda and I went through our photo collection to select a bunch of photos to display Hilary in all her glory, from Day One to today. So many great memories in those photos.

Then we got into the family videos. What a rascal that Hilary was! I'm sorry I didn't take more videos of her—especially her teen years. After she reached high school, the videos are focused on sporting events, but there was so much more I wish I had taped.

I close my eyes and see a beautiful little girl. I open them and see a beautiful young woman. And I have no vision of the years in between. They went by so fast, so very fast.

Yes, I'm sorry Hilary graduated. But I'm also happy for her, proud of her, inspired by her, eager for her to learn and grow at Colgate University.

And we're keeping her room available in our nest, expecting (hoping) she'll fly home often. When she does, we'll do more things together. And I won't need to be sorry anymore.

—*Kennebec Journal* (June 11, 2003)

Chest Pains May Have Saved My Life

A pain in the center of my chest put me in touch with my physician's office a week ago Monday. I thought it was a muscle pull. They took it more seriously.

"Go to the hospital immediately," I was told. That sort of gets your attention.

Arriving at the Augusta emergency waiting room at nine A.M., I found it half full of patients. I signed in, exited to make a few cell-phone calls to cancel scheduled meetings, and then took a seat.

After a few minutes, a woman was wheeled through the waiting room hugging her chest: chest pains. Yikes! She went right into the emergency room for attention. I got a sinking feeling in my stomach.

Eventually my name was called. I provided some basic information and was ushered into a cubicle, attached to machines and an IV line, poked and prodded and told to sit tight while a cardiologist reviewed my blood test results. My blood pressure was soaring and my anxiety was equally high.

I was taken to a room, put into bed, hauled out my briefcase (doesn't everyone take his briefcase to the hospital?), and went to work. They kindly provided me with a bedside phone and I started dialing. Keep the mind occupied.

Then the truly bad news arrived. My troponin level—something produced by the heart—was too high. They would be admitting me and taking more tests. I might have had a heart attack.

At twelve-thirty P.M., stuck in the emergency room and informed that there was, as yet, no room at the inn, I ordered lunch.

Throughout the morning, I asked that my curtain remain open to the entire emergency room. The action in front of me was better than any TV reality show. Organized chaos, I called it, marveling at the cool professionalism of the medical staff. I would not have lasted thirty minutes in that kind of frantic working environment.

I saw all of life pass by me in those five hours. When a battered woman quickly exited the emergency room, too frightened to report her beating to police, the staff took it hard. A mentally unstable child, broken bones, homeless people—it was simply an unbelievable situation with little time for catching one's breath.

At two P.M., upstairs I went to a room with a view. More hookups to machines, poking and prodding, blood and other tests. Things sounded promising. Now focused intently on troponin—something I'd never heard of until that morning—I learned that the troubling high level was somewhat diminished. EKGs looked good. I probably hadn't had a heart attack.

Nurses and other staff were very friendly. My blood pressure went down.

Then I met with cardiologist David Frost, an impressive young guy who expressed an appropriate level of concern about those troponins, and said he recommended an overnight stay so they could be measured a couple more times. Ugh.

After calling Linda at school and ordering up supplies and more reading material, I settled in. A few hours later, with troponins on the rise again, I was moved to the cardiac unit—over my protests. It seemed like a gross overreaction.

But what do I know? In the cardiac unit, I got a private room, nice view of Memorial Bridge, a bigger TV set, and another great group of nurses, one of whom remembered caring for my mom when she was dying of lung cancer.

Brother Gordon, the executive director of the Maine Medical Association, called to assure me the cardiac team that was caring for me was top-notch, but I remained melancholy and anxious, sleeping little. At four A.M. I had a very interesting conversation with my nurse, Ingrid Jenson of Readfield. She lifted my spirits.

By mid-morning, the dreaded troponins were back down and I was sent downstairs for a stress test. It was a piece of cake. I was trotting along on the StairMaster, hardly even puffing, when the cardiologist, Dr. Lesley West, said, "Oh, that doesn't look good. Stop the test."

Trust me, you do not want to flunk your stress test.

Back to the cardiac unit, more talks with my medical team, the scheduling of a more-definitive cardiac catheterization two days hence, and I was cut loose, headed for Mount Vernon where I slept like a baby—up every couple of hours.

Thursday morning I was scrubbed and into the cardiac-catheterization room by nine A.M., where a good discussion of the Red Sox calmed me somewhat. Dr. West was all business, and the catheter was halfway to my heart before I realized it.

No pain but lots of gain, and I watched, fascinated, as a nearby television screen showed the entire process. *There's my heart! I have one! And it's beating!*

About forty-five minutes later, Dr. West pointed out the only flaw—an artery right near the heart that was 80 percent blocked. Nothing else wrong, but almost perfect is not nearly good enough in this situation.

After five hours of recovery, to make sure the artery they used for the catheterization was not bleeding, I was sent home. Then next day the call came. Dr. West explained that a stent should be placed in my artery at that narrow spot.

And so it goes. The pain in my chest remains; it has nothing to do with my heart. I was told it might be a pulled muscle. But I have a feeling it might have saved my life.

—Central Maine Newspapers (September 22, 2004)

Update: A week later the stent was inserted at Maine Medical Center in Portland. I've been good to go ever since.

A Summer Quiz

As we plunge into summer, prepared to endure a flood of friends from away, we ought to be prepared to answer their questions. Here are some of those questions, with answers at the end of the column to help you prepare.

1) We've heard a lot about your governor. How much longer is his term of office?
a) Six months; b) eighteen months; c) too long; d) seems like an eternity.

2) We just saw a bald eagle. Are they:
a) Endangered; b) the state bird; c) eating too many great blue herons; d) year-round residents.

3) What should we see while we are here?
a) Moose; b) Maine Wildlife Park; c) mountains; d) Hermit of Rome's home; e) Maine.

4) Should we retire here?
a) Of course not; b) let's swap homes; c) if you like high taxes; d) there's already too many old people here.

5) Where can we shop?
a) L.L. Bean; b) Goodwill; c) Marden's and Renys; d) yard sales; e) North Conway.

6) Why is your legislature still in session?

a) They heard that Augusta is lovely in the summer; b) they shut down the government, so the governor locked the doors of the Capitol and legislators couldn't get out; c) they did such a poor job in the first six months that they had to repeat that session.

7) We heard that Mainers are heavily armed. Are we safe here?

a) Are you carrying? b) Want to buy a gun?

8) What should we eat here?

a) Blueberry pie, the state dessert; b) whoopie pies, the state treat; c) sardines, which used to be caught and canned here; d) raw milk; e) anything at a farmers' market.

9) What should we do here?

a) Live life the way it should be; b) put on bug spray; c) fasten your seat belt; d) try our microbrews; e) get off the coast; f) spend lots of money.

10) What should we tell our friends when we get home?

a) You loved Maine; b) that the people of Maine are the friendliest you've ever met; c) that Maine is a cheap date; d) that they should visit Maine and be sure to get off the coast.

Feeling So Smart

If you got most of these right, you should be hired at the Welcome to Maine station in Kittery for the summer. Here are the answers.

1) b, c, and d; wishful thinking if you answered six months.
2) b, c, and d. But they spend the winter on the coast.
3) a, b (in Gray, just two minutes from the turnpike—and you can see moose there); c, (yes we have them—get off the coast); d, alas, it's been dismantled; e, the real Maine. Starts north of Augusta.
4) a, b, c, d; feel free to add more good advice.
5) I am sure you can get this one right.
6) I can't give you the answers because I have four legislative bills still in process and can't afford to offend legislators. Oops!
7) Okay, stop having fun and tell them they are safer here than wherever it is that they live.
8) Yes, we are obsessed with sweets: a, b, d, e.
9) b, c, d (definitely), e, and f (please!).
10) Be a billboard for Maine this summer, and spend your own summer vacation right here. We need the money.

—Central Maine Newspapers (May 15, 2013)

Josh Brings the World Home at Christmas

Today Josh begins a long journey home, flying from South Africa to New York, bringing a message that seems most appropriate for Christmas: The best thing in life is serving others.

Our twenty-four-year-old son's East African mission is over for now, but the spirit of service that has already taken him around the world may be his life's work.

Josh took to mission work at Stonehill College, and spent his first postgraduate year serving the homeless in Portland, Oregon. But his story actually starts sooner than that. He had an amazing experience during a "Semester at Sea," when he took college courses while sailing completely around the world, visiting many countries. That experience created in Josh a hankering to explore the world and serve those afflicted with the most devastating poverty and sickness.

In his short life, he has already seen much, from the Indian orphanage of Mother Teresa to the refugee camps of Tanzania, with stops in Japan, China, Vietnam, Brazil, Cuba, and other countries. He seems particularly taken with Africa.

For the past eight months, the last four with his girlfriend Kelly, he has been traveling in East Africa, seeing the sights and volunteering in various missions. It has been a challenging experience, some of which we've been able to share thanks to e-mail.

"I found South Africa to be a very complicated and fascinating country," he reported in one of his first messages last April. "In my mind, things had clearly changed for the better a decade after apartheid, and there is cause for optimism. However, the nation is still divided by race and income; the contrast between gated suburbs and inhumane townships is jarring. The intensity and danger that flows from this reality was somewhat exhausting."

You can imagine how concerned his mother and I have been about Josh's safety, even though we are aware that his planning was meticulous.

In June, Josh joined a team from our own Methodist Church in Readfield to work in a church-sponsored mission in Kaoma, Zambia. When our friends brought back a video of their visit, Josh looked so happy and healthy. We felt much better.

You may read Josh's blog at www.africaisnotacountry. blogspot.com (still available online).

Kelly's e-mails were sometimes heart-wrenching. In Uganda, she taught primary school students. "The children seemed to enjoy their time with me, as each day I was presented with gifts of potatoes, bananas, sugarcane, and the like. These children weren't able to eat breakfast and usually lunch as a result of poverty, yet they found it important to share with me the little they had. An incredibly humbling experience," she wrote.

Classes were crowded (sixty kids in her two sections) and resources very limited. "Such simple things as rain can prevent the students from reaching school, since many walk for miles in each direction to get to school and back home each day," Kelly reported. "In many ways good education is a luxury of rich nations."

While working to address the many problems surrounding them, Josh and Kelly found great peace and beauty in Africa, from Victoria Falls to the island of Lamu, where they wrote, "It was nice that it was safe enough to walk at night, but more than that, it was actually peaceful . . . People seemed even more friendly than normal, with calls of 'Karibou,' or 'You are welcome' following us everywhere."

Josh's insightful reports on the Muslim communities, the AIDS epidemic, political situations, the work of US aid groups, beggars in Malawi, and even the International Criminal Tribunal in Rwanda are remarkable.

Josh and Kelly were thrilled to finally get a permit to visit Josh's friend Watema Emmanuel in a Tanzanian refugee camp, where this young man has been languishing for seven years after fleeing his war-ravaged homeland in the Congo. Watema's story is unbelievable but true. After watching his family members be brutally murdered when the Congo exploded in civil war, Watema escaped, living without food in the woods for days before linking up with an uncle and finding a boat to cross Lake Tanganyika to Tanzania, where he was given a meal and a blue tarp to make his new home, along with hundreds of thousands of other refugees.

Since then, he has seen his sister and her husband die of AIDS, and inherited responsibility for their children. After spending seven years surrounded by the crush of poverty and sickness in his refugee camp, Watema remains amazingly upbeat, hoping to get an education and return to his homeland—something to think about when we review our own wish lists this Christmas.

—Central Maine Newspapers (December 20, 2006)

Texas

In the desert along the Rio Grande River in Big Bend
National Park, in the southwest corner of Texas, we struck
up a conversation with a couple from New Mexico. As soon
as we said we were from Maine, the fellow broke out into a
smile, reporting that every Christmas he calls to order chowder
shipped from Hattie's in Hallowell. It's a small world, isn't it?

The man once lived in Bangor, and the thing he missed
most about Maine was the sound of the white-throated sparrow: *Hel-lo Kimberly Kimberly Kimberly.* When you are birding,
you have many experiences like this.

In the past, I would have said the suggestion that Maine
could expand its tourism economy by attracting birders was
a ridiculous notion. Now, I am one (a birder, not a ridiculous
notion). This was our second trip to Texas to look at birds,
and we left a considerable sum of money scattered along the
birding trail.

Big Bend is high-mountain desert, but I had not paid attention to that as we prepared for the trip by studying our Texas
bird book. And we did see birds—eighty species we could
identify on our own (we are still new to this), with half of
them birds we've never seen before. What I did not antici-
pate was the stunning beauty of the semi-arid desert and
mountains.

Nor did I expect the interesting collection of people and
the quality of food available in the town of Terlingua, a
frankly run-down, dispersed community of nondescript buildings that under ordinary circumstances would have hurried

me along without stopping. I am so very glad we stopped and spent the week there.

We sat on the Terlingua Store porch, where local folks gather every evening to visit, drink beer, and watch the sunset. But they don't face west to watch the sun actually set. They face to the east and watch the sunlight creep up and over the nearby mountains.

We ate world-class barbecued brisket from La Kiva (yes, it's in a cave), the best chili we've ever had at the Starlight, where a fellow entertained us with a complete tour of great old Western songs, and of course, chicken-fried steak (make mine antelope, smothered in a unique beer sauce), again at the Starlight.

And oh, those breakfast burritos at Kathy's Kosmic Kowgirl Kafe. Kathy cooks in a hard-to-miss pink travel trailer while guests eat outside, enjoying what her sign advertised as HEATED DINING in the morning sun, supplemented by a wood fire.

We stayed at Lajitas Resort, where the staff was very friendly and helpful (especially Keith, with his guidance to hot birding spots, and Jim, with his restaurant recommendations). Sitting outside on the patio at the resort's restaurant one evening, feasting on fajitas and enjoying a fine bottle of wine—well, to apply a Maine expression, it was the finest kind.

During our time in Terlingua, Mount Vernon friend Jim Kinney—a Texas native who happened to be there when we were—spent a day with us, bringing along Marty Hanson, a delightful lady who runs the Chihuahuan Desert Research Institute in Fort Davis. We hiked into Pine Canyon, and Marty identified every cactus, flower, and tree, making for a fascinating experience.

An unusual amount of rain had fallen the previous night, and all the cacti were blooming, including one that Marty had never seen blooming in her life. Really exciting stuff!

One of our goals was to see a vermilion flycatcher, a bird with a bright red head and orange body that we'd missed on our Texas trip the year before. The first morning in the park, we went to Cottonwood Campground in Big Bend—and saw fifty vermilions! If you are not a birder, you can't imagine the level of excitement that occurs when you see a bird that you've never seen before in your life.

Texas works to capture birding bucks, with lots of advertising aimed at birders, a wonderful array of maps and brochures, and lots of information on the web that we used to plan our entire trip, even looking at specific hotel rooms before selecting Lajitas Resort's Badlands Hotel.

Maine legislator Bob Duchesne is on the Net, working to create a Maine birding economy. We have our own unique birds, both coastal and inland, and the potential to draw many more birders here. We've already got local characters and great food, but we need infrastructure, targeted marketing, and good place-based information specific to birding. A few vermilion flycatchers wouldn't hurt, either!

—Central Maine Newspapers (May 5, 2010)

Time Sharing at My Brother's Keeper

The adorable little girl shyly looked up at us with bright eyes as her mother said, "She's been waiting all day for you." I complimented the girl on her pretty blue coat, bringing a smile that was more reward than I deserved.

With every delivery of gifts to those in need in the greater Brockton, Massachusetts, area, I received much more than I delivered. Last week I encouraged you to share your abundant resources this Christmas with those who have only abundant needs. That column focused on financial contributions.

Today, I ask you to share something more precious: yourself. Think of this as time sharing. Evaluate each hour of your day. Reallocate as many hours as you can to serving those whose hours are nearly always desperate.

Linda and I, along with daughter Rebekah and grandson Addison, ventured to Brockton this past week to volunteer at My Brother's Keeper, where our son Josh works.

Nineteen years ago Keeper's founders, Jim and Terry Orcutt, answered God's call and made their first Christmas deliveries to fourteen families. This Christmas, Josh, who is in charge of deliveries, and his many volunteer helpers will deliver beautifully wrapped gifts and certificates for Christmas dinners to more than two thousand families.

The program runs on volunteers. Keeper's headquarters in Easton were jammed with volunteers from thirty-eight communities and six states last Saturday. Many were families. Jim and Terry are still front and center, volunteers themselves who have never taken a dime from the program. Their time sharing inspires us all.

Keeper's mission is "to bring the love and hope of Jesus Christ to all we serve." Throughout the year, they deliver furniture, household goods, and food, no charge, to those who seek assistance. There are no prerequisites for service. That's right; there are no background checks, no questions asked, except, "What do you need?" That makes the program fairly unique.

News of Keeper's help spreads by word of mouth, and the program insists only on talking with the applicant by phone. Terry takes a lot of those phone calls herself.

On Saturday morning, after a brief tour of the operation, we settled in at our work table. Daughter-in-law Kelly and her parents, John and Mary Ellen Warch of Long Island, New York, joined us.

A sheet of paper in front of us listed the first names, clothing sizes, and gift lists for a family. Our first was a mother and three kids. Immediately, I recognized that the sheet of paper represented a whole lot more than a Christmas wish list. It was a human needs list, topped by winter hats and gloves. The requests were very modest.

We spread out in the warehouse, searching the shelves of donated items to find the things this family needed, then returning to our table to wrap the gifts and place them in large black bags. After sixty-one years of insisting I was no good at gift wrapping, and proving it every Christmas, God intervened and I learned to wrap. You *can* teach an old dog new tricks!

Keeper's operation is very well organized, and our bags, numbered and labeled, moved to a delivery area where, eventually, they'll be loaded onto a truck (two donated) or van (two loaned) and sent on their way to help improve Christmas celebrations and the lives of those who need that help.

Saturday afternoon John Warch, Linda, and I joined Josh for a delivery run to Taunton. It was humbling, especially for this guy, who has everything he wants. Walk up a flight of stairs into an apartment where a mother struggles to meet the needs of six kids, look into her thankful eyes, and your own Christmas list just might grow a bit smaller.

Imagine how hard it might be to call for help after losing your job, and acknowledging that you can't meet the needs of your family this Christmas. I looked into one guy's eyes and saw that pain.

If you would like to learn more about this great program, you can do that at www.mybrotherskeeper.com. Read Keeper's newsletter, and perhaps it will inspire you to look for a project close to home that needs your help. There are plenty of abundant needs in Maine.

Time sharing in the real estate industry conveys the opportunity to visit a place year after year. Time sharing of the kind I write about today can take you to even better places, whenever you want to go.

—Central Maine Newspapers (December 16, 2009)

Update: For Christmas of 2012, Keeper served over 2,700 families. We go every year now for a weekend before Christmas, to volunteer. It's my favorite Christmas activity. Josh has now been put in charge of opening a new branch of My Brother's Keeper in the Fall River area of Massachusetts. He got it up and running at the end of September 2012.

Finding Christmas

The week of December 5 was hectic. The Christmas rush was beginning to crowd a busy work week—too few hours spent chasing too many tasks. Blood pressure was up, Christmas spirit down.

My work calendar for the Sportsman's Alliance of Maine (SAM) included an all-day meeting of the Maine Outdoor Heritage Fund, two evening meetings of SAM's Fishing Initiative Committee and board of directors, final paste-up of *SAM News*, taping three *Wildfire* television shows, a morning's discussion with GrowSmart and the Brookings Institution, several out-of-town meetings, five thousand words to write, and much more.

Christmas was just twenty-one days away, with pressure building, and I had a couple of Christmas parties that week, plus church choir practice and good intentions to get my shopping done.

And then, on Tuesday, my father-in-law died. Lewis Hillier of Winthrop was eighty-five, a quiet and modest World War II veteran who earned a Purple Heart on the front lines at the Battle of the Bulge, a man whose legacy is his family. He and his wife Ivy raised seven great children, the youngest of whom is my wife Linda.

Suddenly my week changed. Things that once seemed important vanished from my schedule. The only task was a new one not in my original work plan: I had to write and deliver Lew's eulogy. That was a privilege.

The change in plans caused me to think about the important things in life, and to contemplate Christmas in a very different light. Not the bright lights that dominate this season, but the soft lights that illuminate the soul. It was time to look inward, and Lew's death provided that luxury.

I found Christmas in my woodlot during an afternoon's hike, spruce trees sporting snowy blankets (now I know what "spruced-up" means!). A deer grazed among acorns, scarcely noticing my presence. Hopkins Stream, with shoulders of frozen ice reflecting a brilliant sun, was barely moving along.

Gazing north, I noticed a beaver in midstream, headed my way. I hunkered down behind a tree and he swam on by, intent on completing his own chores. If I had been on the stream in my canoe, he would have slapped his tail on the water, angered by my presence in his domain. On this day, I was part of his environment, not a threat to it. After he passed, I sat entranced by the ice—calm, content.

A small head poked out of the snowy branches not twenty feet away and an ermine pranced out, already white after shedding his brown summer coat, perhaps the only one truly ready for winter. He scampered away toward a nearby ridge, never even glancing my way, so tiny, so fierce.

South of me in the stream, a dozen ducks—buffleheads—bobbed in the water's surface, and yonder hill could have been a backdrop for anyone's favorite Christmas card.

Here was the Christmas tableau I sought, the place where God always speaks to me. That afternoon, he helped rearrange my schedule to focus on the special season that Christmas can be—and usually is not.

The irony is that we all know what to do to make Christmas special—but we usually do just the opposite. Wishing for peace, we go for packages. Needing calm, we fill the schedule with clamor.

Having cleared my schedule in the first week of December to honor my father-in-law, I got out a pen and slashed through the rest of December's chores. Only the most important survived. I wanted my search for Christmas to continue. And I was going to be stubborn about it.

Despite pleas from my family, I refused to prepare a wish list of gifts I wanted to find under the tree on Christmas morning. Something thoughtful, something simple, I murmured. Looks of disbelief did not deter me.

Last Saturday night, with daughter Hilary, I sang Handel's *Messiah* with the community at South Parish Church in Augusta, accompanied by the Augusta Symphony Orchestra. I had planned to attend a basketball game—but there will be plenty of them in the months to come.

This sing-along set just the right tone for my inspired version of Christmas 2005: splendid, enthusiastic, loving, spiritual. The last time I sang the *Messiah* was with my mother at a large Catholic church in Lewiston. Mom has been gone five years, but her presence was strong on Saturday night at South Parish Church.

This new, relaxed Christmas—focused on church activities, music, scaled-down expectations for gifts, more time with family members—is a final gift from Lew. While mourning him, I managed to find Christmas.

—Central Maine Newspapers (December 21, 2005)

New Year's Resolutions

New Year's resolutions should be frivolous. That seems to be the position of my immediate family. Josh, Hilary, and Linda grow increasingly frustrated each year by my New Year's Day demand that we each prepare resolutions for the coming twelve months.

I urge. I plead. I admonish. And sometimes I prepare the resolutions for them. I have also kept these resolutions in a file since 1990. Back then, the resolutions had more resolve.

For example, Hilary used a crayon at age six to make her list, which included the following: "Resilutions: get all S's on report cards, try to read 50 books, try to write one paragraf a day, do one math paper a day (not counting school)." She was obviously focused on school!

But Hilary also included that year, "Use the microwave 11 times or more, do not act up in publick, no pouting, and no skreeming at Mom and Dad."

By 1994, although the screaming went on, these later resolutions had disappeared from Hilary's list, apparently recognizing that it takes more than a sheet of paper on New Year's Day to change human behavior. Hilary's 1994 list was remarkably brief: "Put my bike together and be able to ride it, read at least 53 books, learn to type." That was a lot more realistic. She completed all three.

Joshua caught on to the program early. The oldest list of resolutions in my file for Josh include, "Get better at basketball, get better at soccer, get better at baseball, and get another 2,000 baseball cards." But he didn't ignore the human

element, resolving to "help Mom and not tease my sister."
Curiously, no resolution to "help Dad." Josh also resolved to
"try to get my mom to let me stay up later," and "try to get a
higher allowance."

Finally, I knew he was on to me with the last resolution that
year, to "not do resilutions next year."

By 1994 Josh was neatly typing his resolutions, some of
which were turning into lifetime listings. Among Josh's resolutions for '94 were "to get better at basketball, baseball, soccer,
and Ping-Pong." Well, at least we had a new sport there. Josh's
demands had soared, though, as he was hoping to "get at least
3,500 more baseball cards."

Of course, he tossed in a few to please Dad, like "get high
honors every quarter," and "get to be a better cook," but it did
not take a genius to notice that I was beginning to lose him,
in the resolutions that promised to "tease my sister more," and
"have fun!" Resolutions are not supposed to be fun.

Last year Josh took out after me with a vengeance, listing a
total of twenty-seven resolutions. Many were outstanding, setting high goals for schoolwork, music, and sports. I especially
liked the ones about fishing, which included, "get better at fly
fishing" and "catch over a sixteen-inch fish."

He did get a lot better at fly fishing, and caught the season's
largest fish, a fourteen-and-a-half-inch wild brook trout. Probably I'll see a sixteen-inch goal again on his 1996 list. He also
accomplished many of his other resolutions, including "beat
Dad at Ping-Pong," and there were the usual new goals for
baseball cards, books, and games.

The perennial was there, too: "Tease my sister more," with
new resolutions "to be able to get my sister to shut up when

I tell her to," and "get my sister to stop doing that thing with her eyeballs." Honestly, I have no idea what the latter is all about, but the shutting up went unaccomplished.

Lin steadfastly refuses to join in this resolution exercise, although I do prepare a few for her every year. In 1993 she actually verbalized four resolutions that I quickly set down on paper, and I notice in reviewing them that she achieved all but one. She still doesn't "spend at least one hour each day relaxing and doing something special for herself."

For me, I develop resolutions in a feverish desire for improvement and accomplishment. Diet and exercise appear each year on the list, and there are other perennials that, for one reason or another, are never achieved and hence carried forward. Sometimes they are masked in new language, like "eat more nutritiously and less voluminously" (1993), but they are all the same, really.

"Paint the back of the house" first appeared on my list in 1991. It'll be there again in 1996, I'm sorry to report. "Spend more time training the dog" appears each year, too, as does the plan to build a hiking/skiing trail through our woodlot.

For the sake of appearances, I usually list "Keep the kitchen clean for Lin," or "Learn how to cook." In 1994 I resolved to master our new computer system (who am I kidding?), plant a new lawn on the west side of the house (nope), and spend time fishing the Kennebec River with Dad (we went once).

And of course, I resolved to "complete all 1993 resolutions." Fanatically frivolous, wouldn't you say?

—*Kennebec Journal* (1995)

What Can Church Do for You?

The steady beep of a backing UPS truck drew my gaze out the window and away from the computer screen, and I stepped to the door to await the delivery of a package.

What can Brown do for you? Deliveries right to my doorstep in Mount Vernon, for starters. Their slogan must be one of the all-time best—it stays with you, stuck somewhere in the brain where it just can't be dislodged.

It was still there, bouncing around, while I sat in church the following Sunday. "What can Brown do for you?" I wondered. That was followed quickly by a better thought: "What can *church* do for you?"

Inasmuch as Pastor Karen Munson was just beginning a thought-provoking sermon, I had to set aside the question for pondering at a later date.

This is that date.

Church can bring music into your life. My mom was the organist and choir director at the Winthrop Methodist Church, so of course I was in the youth choir. To this day, singing in the church choir remains an inspirational activity for me.

Although known as a hunter and angler, there is nothing that's more fun for me than Thursday-night choir practices led by Jeff Munson. Pianist John Twitchell is an amazing talent, so we can tackle lively and challenging music. Singing at church services is fun, too, but we only get to sing one piece each Sunday, while on Thursdays, it's an hour of singing a variety of great songs. That just can't be beat.

Church can offer a lifetime of memories: the good, the somber, the inspirational. Lin and I married in the Jesse Lee Methodist Church on top of the hill in Readfield, the oldest Methodist Church in Maine, and a beautiful building. Although the wedding was heavenly, it was as hot as hell that day, well over 100 degrees. It was a lifetime memory in all respects.

My mom's funeral—moved to the Catholic Church in Winthrop to accommodate a crowd eight hundred strong—was a somber memory that stays with me, many parts of it still vivid.

One favorite memory wasn't at a service, but a church supper. Seated at our table was our then-pastor George Darling. Daughter Hilary, age three, turned to Pastor Darling and asked, "God, please pass the Jell-O." We're still laughing about that one seventeen years later.

Church can be a refuge. Prayer time is just one point in the service when you can lift your concerns to God, who always listens. You can actually feel your burdens lifting from your shoulders as you share them with God and the congregation. And there are times when, alone in that sanctuary, you can feel the safety and security of God's arms around you.

Church can give you a chance to serve. Our Readfield Methodist Church serves people around the globe and in the neighborhood. Lynn Twitchell's African project draws many of us into the global world of needs, and the Mount Vernon food bank reminds us that some of those needs are close to home. We're a giving church, but in truth, you get more than you give, always.

Church can make you think, ponder your place in the world, challenge you to greater good, and even give you an idea for a newspaper column! We are blessed by a pastor whose sermons are both insightful and inspirational. After a week in which my focus is intensely on the issues that are critical to sportsmen, it's nice to focus, even if only for an hour or two, on the issues that are critical to God.

Church can surround you with people who love and care about you—and not just on Sunday. Anyone who is ill or otherwise in need of care is fortunate indeed to be a part of our caring congregation. There isn't room in this brief column to list those who have brought that care into our lives and the lives of so many others—and most importantly, even to those who are not members of our congregation. They reach out to you on a daily basis.

Our Christmas Fair brings this home for me every year. It's so much more than a fund-raiser. It's a tradition of sharing and caring, laughter, song, food, and Christmas cheer. It inspires us, in a season that can be miserable for many, to focus on the birth of Jesus and what that means for us, rather than on what may be stocked on the shelves at our favorite store.

Of course, I must be honest here: I am often found at the Christmas Fair, focusing on the food table. Wow, do we have some great cooks in our church! Nona Boyink's two-berry pie is scrumptious beyond words. This year I purchased two of them (and I sure hope my cardiologist isn't reading this column).

What can church do for you? Perhaps it's time to find out.

—Central Maine Newspapers (February 1, 2006)

About the Author
George Arthur Smith

I am sometimes introduced as a "troublemaker," the person Graham Greene was describing in *The Quiet American* when he wrote, "I never knew a man who had better motives for all the trouble he caused."

Public service and politics have been my career, I suppose, if I even had a career, but all of my jobs required writing and speaking skills, and it's the writing that's been my favorite activity. So I've spent a lot of time doing it, learning to write well by . . . well, by writing. It's helped that, since I was a little kid, I've had my head in a book. I love to read.

In 1989 Doug Rooks recruited me to write a weekly editorial-page column in the *Kennebec Journal*, which morphed into a weekly column in 1991. The column was added to the *Waterville Morning Sentinel* about ten years ago. Most of the columns in this book first appeared there.

Occasionally someone will ask, "How could you possibly come up with a column idea every week?" My response is always, "Are you kidding? Do you read a daily newspaper? Something pisses me off every day!"

It's kind of difficult to summarize my work history, but it goes something like this: 1970s, Congressman David Emery's staff; 1980s, campaign consulting business; 1990s and 2000s, executive director of the Sportsman's Alliance of Maine. But this doesn't really even begin to describe all the interesting things I got into, such as writing comprehensive plans for small rural towns. I've always been a strong advocate for rural Maine.

I grew up in the small town of Winthrop, graduated from the University of Maine in Orono, and have lived with my wife Linda in the very small Mount Vernon since 1979. Linda is a first-grade teacher.

My political work was all-Republican for most of my life. I was Bill Cohen's driver on his first campaign for Congress, and managed Dave Emery's first campaign for Congress, working with Dave during his eight years as Maine's First District Congressman. This was back when politics was fun. I left the Republican reservation to help Angus King get elected governor in 1995.

I was born a Maine sportsman, raised a Maine sportsman, and will die a Maine sportsman. This year it is a very special privilege to be hunting and fishing for the fifty-third year with my ninety-year-old dad. After serving on the board of directors and as president of the Sportsman's Alliance of Maine in the late 1970s and early 1980s, I returned to active duty in 1993 when SAM fell on hard times. The plan was to fix things and move on, but I loved the job and stuck with it for eighteen years, retiring at the end of 2010 to write full-time.

Ah yes, I have done a bit of writing. A monthly column in *The Maine Sportsman* magazine for almost forty years. The weekly editorial-page column for central Maine's daily newspapers for twenty-two years. Lots of columns for lots of newsletters, including 15,000 to 20,000 words for each issue of the *SAM News*. And now my favorite assignment: weekly travel columns with my wife Linda, published in the *Kennebec Journal* and *Morning Sentinel*.

I've done a bit of talking too, including twelve years as
cohost, with my friend Harry Vanderweide, of *Wildfire,* a
TV talk show focused on hunting, fishing, conservation, and
environmental issues. It is currently owned and produced by
Maine Audubon, and can be accessed on their website, as well
as the Time Warner cable station throughout Maine.

In 1983 I was part of the management team that successfully defended Maine's moose hunt in a referendum campaign.
I also managed a successful 1982 campaign that placed the
Department of Inland Fisheries and Wildlife in the Maine
Constitution, and protected its revenue. And I led (with my
sister Edie) a successful campaign in 2004 to defeat an animal
rights group's referendum to stop Maine's bear hunt.

The best idea I ever had was the Maine Outdoor Heritage
Fund. With the support of then-governor Angus King, and a
strong partnership between Maine Audubon and the Sportsman's Alliance of Maine, we created the Outdoor Heritage Fund,
funded by an instant lottery game that has now provided over
$17 million in grants for wildlife conservation and outdoor rec-
reation projects. I loved serving on the MOHF board for its first
ten years, until I got tossed aside by term limits.

Along the trail I've managed to serve five years as a member of the Winthrop Town Council, three years as a Mount
Vernon selectman, three years as a Kennebec County Commissioner, nine years on the Mount Vernon Planning Board,
and thirty-three years as a trustee of the Dr. Shaw Memorial
Library—my favorite job, mostly because I get a key to the
library and can go there anytime I want.

It's also been my privilege to serve on many state task
forces and advisory committees, including the Forest Legacy

Advisory Committee, the Hatchery Commission, and the Great Ponds Task Force. Lots of studies and good recommendations; not much action on them.

Back in the day, Harry Vanderweide—Maine's best-known sportsman, longtime editor of *The Maine Sportsman* magazine, and host of his own hunting and fishing TV show for more than twenty years—delivered a memorable (for me) and astonishing (for everyone else) tribute. It went like this:

> To mix metaphors, Smith is a political gadfly and human dynamo who is impressive for the sheer volume of work he turns out. Without doubt, Smith is the most effective sportsman-lobbyist this state has ever seen. He has a great deal of personal power for a lot of reasons, including being a political columnist for *The Maine Sportsman*, a daily newspaper columnist, a television news personality, and the executive director of the Sportsman's Alliance of Maine.
>
> Although he has been known in the past as a conservative political organizer and fund-raiser, Smith is metamorphosing into a consensus-builder for the diverse groups who fall under the general umbrella of "sportsmen." His strengths include access to Maine's total political structure, and his ability to turn abstract concepts into politically achievable action. Smith is the man who can most take credit for turning SAM from a path of slow dissolution to the fastest-growing political force in Maine, in just one short year.

Thanks, Harry!

If I've accomplished anything major, it is this: Rebekah, Joshua, and Hilary—my children. I am so proud of each one of them. I could write a book about them. Hey, maybe I will!